W/19
S

ADVANCE PRAISE FOR
MODERN LUNCH **BY ALLISON DAY**

"Looks like breakfast is going to have to relinquish its title, lunch is now The Most Important Meal of the Day. Every page of Allison's book, *Modern Lunch*, is so fresh, inventive, and downright mouthwatering, I find myself just counting down the minutes until the clock strikes noon!"
ROSIE DAYKIN, owner of Butter Baked Goods and author of *Butter Baked Goods*, *Butter Celebrates!*, and *Let Me Feed You*

"Is it possible that Allison has just made lunch—the chore of all chores for a parent like me—the most exciting meal of the day? This book is bursting with flavor, inspiration, and, most of all, encouragement to make the midday meal something to savor."
CERI MARSH, co-author of *How to Feed a Family* and *The School Year Survival Cookbook*

"*Modern Lunch* is an absolutely brilliant cookbook. Each recipe feels globally inspired and yet lovingly curated for the home cook. Sign me up for Allison's Modern Lunch Club because I predict that lunch is soon to be my new favourite meal."
AIMÉE WIMBUSH-BOURQUE, food blogger and author of *The Simple Bites Kitchen* and *Brown Eggs and Jam Jars*

Modern Lunch
Allison Day

+ 100 Recipes for Assembling
the New Midday Meal

appetite
by RANDOM HOUSE

Appetite by Random House® and colophon are registered trademarks of
Penguin Random House LLC.

Library and Archives of Canada Cataloguing in Publication is available
upon request.
ISBN: 978-0-14-753100-1
eBook ISBN: 978-0-14-753101-8

Cover and book design: Jennifer Griffiths
Cover and book photography: All photographs by Allison Day except
pages 150, 151, 178, 179, 182, 183, and author photograph, which are by
Geoff Woodley.
Printed and bound in China

Published in Canada by Appetite by Random House®,
a division of Penguin Random House Canada Limited.

www.penguinrandomhouse.ca

10 9 8 7 6 5 4 3 2 1

For Geoff, full of adventure,
patience, and positivity.

Contents

Introduction

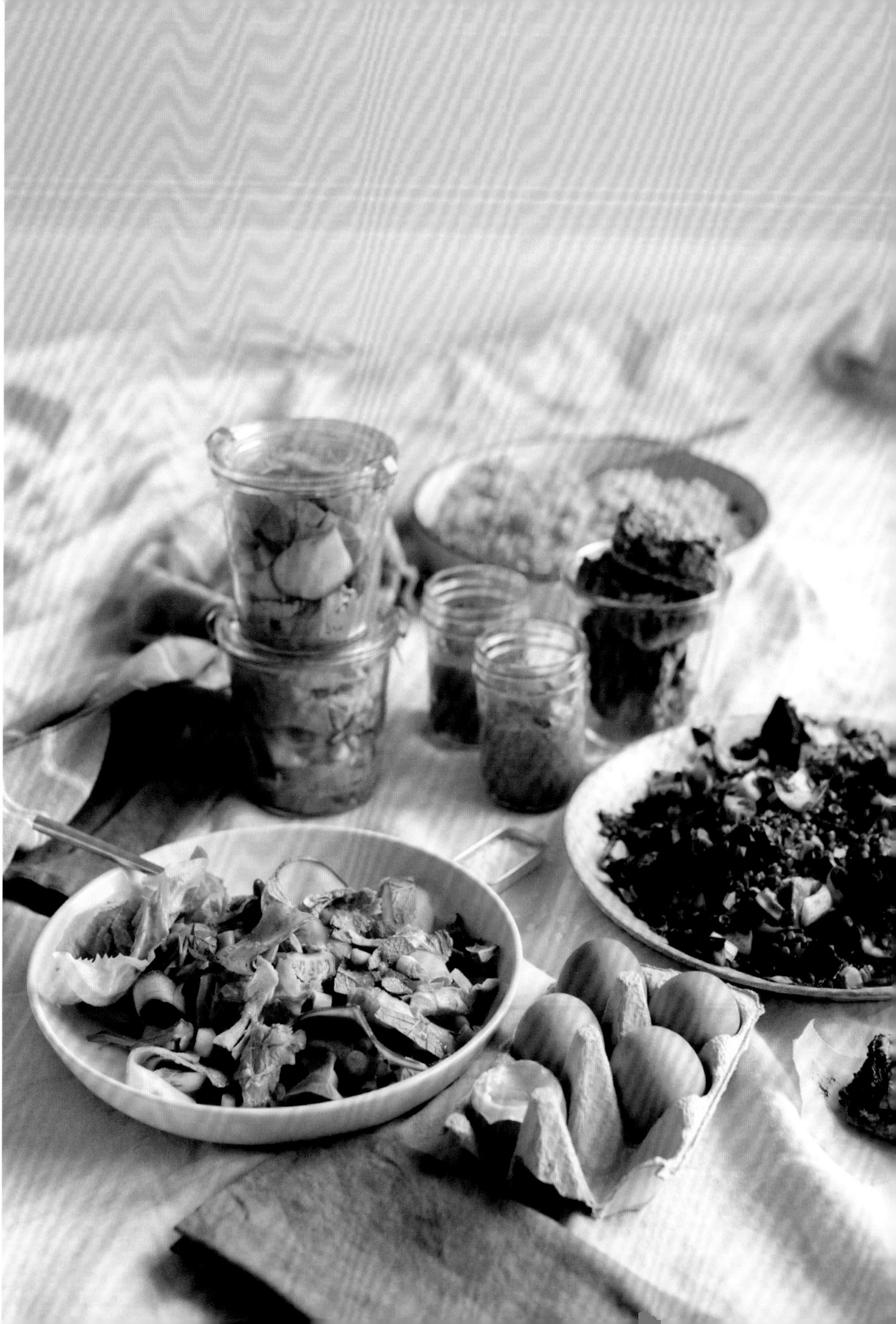

LIFE IS TOO SHORT to eat a bad lunch. Yet, in our culture, the midday meal is a forgotten opportunity to reinvigorate ourselves with food that makes us happy and energized. It has to be fairly quick and easy, and that often means resorting to convenience foods. There seems to be no middle ground: it's either buy lunch or pack something sad. So I'm here to help you formulate and practice new rituals (I know some of you are already on your way!) to make homemade, balanced, and delicious lunches materialize. I'm not suggesting that you have to cook a from-scratch, freshly prepared sit-down meal every day—it can be just as special when prepped ahead (your new "leftovers"), especially with a touch more attention and creativity put into the ingredients used, presentation, and packing than what we're used to. I promise, the reclamation of lunch is simple!

Like most kids, I found discovering what was in my packed school lunch a thrill. My parents would send me to school with sandwiches of iceberg lettuce, cheddar cheese, and mayonnaise on squishy whole-wheat sandwich bread, alternating only with peanut butter and honey or peanut butter and banana (which I still really enjoy). After the main course, there was always a treat of some kind, usually a small bag of cookies or chips, and a piece of fruit. And it was all stowed away in worn (clean yet always oddly cloudy) plastic containers that circulated between my older brother, me, and finally my younger sister, until they were retired to the recycling bin when they became officially too warped to snap shut.

As my eating preferences have changed, so have my lunches. However, the midday meal continues to have a hint of delicious nostalgia for me, not simply for the food but for the community it builds. Breakfast and dinner are often family affairs, while lunch is a break in our day when most of us are connecting with friends, colleagues, or someone who happens to be enjoying their meal on the same park bench. I've made friends with strangers by simply asking, "What's for lunch?"

Lunch is a meal that needs a fresh coat of paint, a meal that deserves the same respect dinner receives, while still embracing the casualness of breakfast. To me, the story of lunch as it's enjoyed today has yet to be told. Yes, it's a break in the day to replenish the body and mind, even if you're devouring a cup of noodles "al desko," an *Oxford English Dictionary*-defined word (you're welcome!). It's a way to travel and taste a range of global flavors, all without a plane ticket. A homemade lunch saves you money, helps you eat healthier (made easier still with the recipes in this book), and gives you a swift boost to reenergize your day. And it's a meal where the lighting is just so perfect for capturing a photo to share on Instagram (I do, @allisondaycooks). But it can be more than this, too. I'd like to introduce you to the "modern lunch."

A modern lunch is special, simple, (mostly) make-ahead, healthy, share-worthy, community building, money saving, colorful, and delicious. It culls inspiration from world cuisines, is adaptable to your personal taste and pantry, and is always satisfying. It can be enjoyed at your desk, in the lunchroom, on a bench outside, at home, on the road, on a picnic blanket, in the car, at a set table, or on your lap in front of the TV. A modern lunch can be about connectedness: it's a time to put yourself out there, socialize, and make new friends or bond with old ones. Done with intention and meaning, the modern lunch should get you excited about a quality midday meal!

As you join me in reimagining the idea of lunch, think of this cookbook as your textbook. The meals here are healthier, tidier, travel better, and will satisfy not only your palate more than a sandwich but also your mood, leaving you with sustained energy as opposed to a deep dive into the afternoon slump post-PB&J. I'm celebrating fresh produce, quality proteins, healthy fats, and interesting whole grains. You can even start a Modern Lunch Club at your work or school: cook once a week for the group and enjoy a range of recipes the rest of the week without lifting a finger (just a fork or spoon) (see page 205 for details).

And in our busy lives, there's often little time to devote to a just-made meal, especially at lunch. Because of this, many of the recipes you'll find in *Modern Lunch* pack beautifully, require minimal prep for myriad lunches, and are all made with ingredients you can find wherever you're located.

But an unpacked lunch, such as lunch at home on workdays, also happens, more so for some than others. Those of us who find ourselves at home during lunch—the large percentage of the population who work from home, including at-home parents, people on maternity or paternity leave, shift workers who have a week off, or any number of other positions—need grab-and-go options to get us through our days. We don't have food trucks lined up outside our doors, and if you live in the countryside, as I did growing up, or the suburbs, the only alternative to a homemade lunch is usually fast food. Still, working from home doesn't give you the time to make a from-scratch meal every day,

which is why I advocate for, and guide you toward doing meal prep and turning to make-ahead lunches. Weekends are a completely different story, though: on these days, lunch at home can mean a sit-down brunch, steaming-hot midday spread, multi-salad event, or picnic banquet. The weekend is an occasion to put a little extra panache into the midday meal—and we get to celebrate it once a week, all year long.

I have the readers of my first cookbook *Whole Bowls* and my food blog *Yummy Beet* to thank for putting a lunch cookbook in my mind. The make-ahead, meal prep, choose-your-own-adventure aspect of *Whole Bowls* was perfect for packed lunches, and when I saw your photos on social media of packed lunches and weekend "leftover" bowls, the idea of *Modern Lunch* was born.

Because I'm in a living situation where I'm getting both sides of the coin on weekdays (I work from home and my partner, Geoff, heads out the door every morning to work), I knew I needed to create meals that would add some zest to both of our days, whether they were enjoyed out of a container or on a plate. I wanted make-ahead or assembly-only recipes for myself, while he wanted salads that are made to last (i.e., can be thrown in a container and

then tossed haphazardly in a bag without exploding, and can hang around without getting soggy) and one-dish deals that can be zapped quickly or enjoyed cold. Oh, and did I mention we're both food-obsessed home cooks? We want explosive flavor! One-pot meals are our go-to during the cooler months, satisfying both the at-home and to-go crowd. In the heat of summer, plant-centered salads that can keep—even already dressed—for days in the refrigerator, like the Sunday Kale Salad (page 131), are always on the menu; just throw some prepped protein on top (I've given you many ideas for simple protein add-ons in the Modern Meal Prep Staples chapter to help you out; see page 235), then pack for later or dive in immediately.

While writing and thinking about this cookbook, and talking with family and friends, two questions kept coming up:

1 WHY CAN'T I JUST PACK UP LAST NIGHT'S DINNER?
You absolutely can! But maybe you were very hungry and ate the entire meal. Maybe you went out for dinner or had takeout. Don't always count on dinner for lunch is all I'm trying to get across here. If you do have leftovers, which doesn't always happen, they don't necessarily reheat or carry over to the following day well. Most of the recipes in this book are built to last a few days at a minimum, are assembled in a way that preserves freshness, and may not even need reheating. It's about treating lunch as you do breakfast and dinner—as its own thing.

My position is definitely unconventional in today's world, but it works by creating a new, healthy cooking habit around lunch: the habit of preparing efficiently ahead of time. This habit will flow into other meals you cook, too, producing a greater passion and appreciation for homemade food overall.

2 WHY AREN'T THERE ANY SANDWICH RECIPES IN THIS BOOK?
It didn't start out this way. I thought they needed to be included. It was Geoff who said, "I don't read a cookbook to learn how to make a sandwich." He had a point. (Though there are many good cookbooks wholly dedicated to the subject that I can recommend to you, if you really want to expand your lunchtime recipe repertoire.) When I want a sandwich for lunch, I make one, eat it, and love it, but it's not an everyday thing for me. (If you're wondering, my sandwich favorites include a really good BLT or simply toasted summer tomato and mayo, egg salad,

grilled chicken club, peanut butter and banana, and a California veggie–style sandwich with loads of avocado. If Geoff is cooking, it's got to be grilled cheese, and I'll make tomato soup to pair with that. So, now you know.)

My cooking style has grown with me through (now) three books, traversing different cities, dietary preferences, and kitchens of all shapes and sizes, including a kitchen in a 530-square-foot flat in London, England. What's remained constant are that my recipes are heavy on the produce, with proteins and grains to complement. And I still favor creating and eating meals that are adaptable to any mood, diet, and grocery situation. Mixing, matching, or replacing proteins, grains, and vegetables will ensure that everyone will find something appealing. These are methods, meals, and life strategies to help you carve out a new way of healthy eating and living, one that nourishes your body and spirit while enhancing your lifestyle, if only for a few hours a day.

Whether you eat at home, at work, at play, or on the road, you'll find something in here to relish the midday meal in a real-life manner. *Modern Lunch* skips the drama of dinner and mercurial moods of breakfast, showcasing meals that are never too much but more than enough to drive you through the rest of your day.

This is my idea of lunch, and I'm eager to know yours. Let's create our own modern lunch, together.

How to Make Lunch Happen

Lunchtime Success Tips

Keep It Fresh

Keep your chopped, cooked, and prepped-ahead foods fresh all week by following these simple storage tips. This means no more dry grains, gray meats, or desiccated crudités.

PRODUCE

Cut-up Raw Vegetables
Separate into individual airtight containers; cover with cold water to stop from drying out. Refrigerate.

Roasted Vegetables
Separate into individual airtight containers. Refrigerate.

PROTEIN

Cooked Poultry, Meat, Fish, and Tofu
Separate each kind into individual airtight containers. Refrigerate.

Hard-boiled Eggs
Store in a bowl or save an egg carton to devote to hard-boiled eggs; if using the carton, be sure to label it with an "HB" to avoid confusion with your fresh eggs. Refrigerate.

GRAINS

All Cooked Whole Grains
Separate each kind into individual airtight containers. Refrigerate.

Pasta and Noodles
Toss with olive oil, and then separate each kind into individual airtight containers. Refrigerate.

CONDIMENTS

Separate each kind into individual airtight containers or jars. Refrigerate.

Master Meal Prep

Meal prep is making ahead whole recipes or recipe components for easy assembling and packing of lunches throughout the week. Take a few hours each week (I like Sunday afternoons) to shop, chop, cook, and stash your freshly prepared foods for fantastic made-by-you lunches and snacks all week long. Check out the Modern Meal Prep Staples chapter to get started (page 235).

PLAN THIS WEEK'S LUNCH MENU You have a few possibilities for that, and here they are:

1 **BY THE BOOK** Cook 2 to 4 full main course recipes and 1 or 2 snack recipes, like Cold Noodle Salad with Smoked Tofu and Miso-Sesame Dressing (page 25) and Spanish Lentils with Olives, Almonds, and Saffron (page 55), along with Ginger Kombucha–Baked Rhubarb Yogurt Parfaits (page 230) and one of the Power Snacks (page 218).

2 **STAPLE-STYLE** You can't go wrong with a few classic meal prep staples to make your lunch—these recipes keep it simple with minimal ingredients. Choose 1 grain, 1 protein, 2 vegetables, and 1 dressing from the Modern Meal Prep Staples chapter (page 235) to assemble in a container, like a grain bowl to go. For example, build a lunch of quinoa, canned tuna, Green Goddess Dressing (page 237), a handful of arugula, and roasted vegetables. Any of the Savory and Sweet No-Recipe Snack Solutions (page 224), most of which take less than 2 minutes to assemble, are easy, healthy options for when you feel peckish.

3 **CUSTOMIZED** Construct a main course out of a handful of different full recipes' components for your very own signature lunch. For example, combine the squash agrodolce from the Squash Agrodolce on Yogurt with Dukkah (page 168) with the zucchini noodles from the Zucchini Tangle with Romesco and Burrata (page 133) or the poached chicken from the Modern Meal Prep Staples (page 235) with honey-mustard dressing from Greens and Farro with Chicken, Avocado, and Honey-Mustard Dressing (page 135). For snacking, buy or make a batch of Nut Butter (page 237) to enjoy with apple slices, or add a dollop on top of the Express Chocolate Pudding Cups (page 215) for a luxurious twist.

4   MIX AND MATCH   Try 1 full main course recipe and supplement with 2 or 3 staple recipes, along with a snack. This could look like Cauliflower Fatteh with Pine Nuts and Dates (page 40) paired with roasted vegetables and hard-boiled eggs from the Modern Meal Prep Staples (page 235), and for snacking, the Berry and Apple Oat Squares (page 216).

SHOP ONCE   Now that you've chosen the recipes, make a grocery list with the fresh ingredients you'll need for the week. Most of the staple ingredients used in these recipes (which you may find in your kitchen right now), like grains, oils, vinegars, canned beans, yogurt, cheeses, proteins, and more, will translate into your usual dinnertime cooking, so there's no need to stock up specifically for lunch. I'm saving you time *and* money! Just remember, before you leave the house, check your ingredient stash twice, and shop once.

SCHEDULE COOKING   If you're used to going out for lunch every day, this step can be the hardest, so please be patient. After the first month, you won't know how you ever did without a home-made lunch—for a couple of days during the workweek, at least.

A homemade lunch won't happen if you don't make it happen. Devoting just a few hours of cooking per week, a lot of which is hands-off time as you wait for your proteins to roast, eggs to boil, grains to rehydrate, vegetables to soften, and one-pot meals to stew, will make assembling lunch *à la minute* that much easier. The "hard" part is done. All that's left to do is pack it all up.

Many people, myself included, find Sunday the best day to schedule a few hours for meal prep. You may need to replenish on Wednesdays, depending on how many people require lunch.

Meal prepping may seem like a lot of work up front, but the more hands in the kitchen, the faster it goes. And the results pay off big-time. If you have a partner, a housemate, or kids, get them involved. Their incentive is food, of course! Put on music or a podcast, which makes the activity more fun—I personally can't cook without them. If you prefer flashier entertainment, run your favorite TV show or movie in the background.

SCHEDULE LUNCH   Lunch happened when we were kids because it was scheduled, and many workplaces function this way, too. If you're working over your lunch break, which I tend to do, remember to eat something good!

And if you're new to homemade lunches, don't worry. Start slowly and aim to bring 1 homemade lunch to work the first week, 2 the second week, and so on, until you have as many days of packed lunches as you desire.

FIND YOUR FAVORITE STAPLES Use the Modern Meal Prep Staples (page 235) for grains, proteins, and condiments you can keep in the refrigerator all week long for quick assembly of lunch to go or at home. Think about your ideal salad bar, one with everything you love, and choose your lunch staple recipes based on that.

PARE DOWN AMOUNTS Stick to a couple of complete lunch recipes per week to avoid being overwhelmed. Additionally, choose 3 to 5 basics (see Modern Meal Prep Staples, page 235) to have on hand. Even if you're cooking for just yourself, batch-cooking once will ensure that you eat many times.

STORE IT WELL You're going to need something to store your prepared items in. I use large containers or covered bowls for prepared grains, proteins, and vegetables, and find that liquid dressings or condiments are best kept in airtight glass jam jars.

USE REAL DISHES AND UTENSILS (OPTIONAL)
This is an optional tip because there are so many instances when this doesn't apply, such as if you want to use the beautiful and practical lunch containers that can fully replace real dishes and utensils (see the Gear Guide for ideas, page 245).

If you prefer to eat your packed lunch outside its travel container, I recommend going to IKEA and buying yourself a few new lunch dishes: a small bowl (for snacks and side dishes), a large bowl (for big salads, grain bowls, stews, and entrée soups), a small plate, a large plate, and a set of inexpensive stainless steel cutlery. If you have extras of these at home or can find them on a thrifting adventure, even better. Write your name on the bottoms of your dishes in permanent marker if you're worried about workplace "borrowing."

EMBRACE THE FREEZER Take a few minutes to separate portions of prepared, freezer-friendly meals. The best recipes for freezing are easy to find with the Modern Lunch freezer-friendly icon (see page 14). Leave 1 to 2 inches of empty space at the top of the container, as frozen meals, like soups or stews, expand when frozen, which can crack your container if it's too full. Label the container with masking tape and a permanent marker, noting the dish, date, and serving size.

WAKE UP LEFTOVERS A good number of the recipes in *Modern Lunch* were created to taste stellar even when they're made in advance and eaten fridge-cold. But sometimes a little pick-me-up is needed to bring out the best in chilled, already prepared food.

Right before serving, try squeezing a wedge of fresh lemon or lime over your meal (this is highly therapeutic) or drizzling it with balsamic vinegar. You can also toss in some fresh herbs like basil or mint, and reseason with salt. Even a few dots of hot sauce can give a small but mighty kick to your meal.

BUILD A WORKPLACE PANTRY You will not regret this, though you may be met with quizzical stares. Your workplace flavor pantry basics include salt, hot sauce, balsamic vinegar, tamari, crackers, canned sardines, and natural almond butter or peanut butter (be sure to refrigerate nut butters). The pantry can be a desk drawer, small basket in the common kitchen, or a take-along kit that you bring with you every day.

Recipe Legend

Note these minor yet important details in every recipe; the more you use this book, the more you'll see how helpful these details are. At the top of each recipe are helpful icons to tell you at a glance if a recipe is packable, will need reheating, is make-ahead friendly, and is suitable for the freezer.

Many recipes are accompanied by Lunch Notes, a brief tip or two to guide you through everything from restyling your meal for a new presentation to ingredient buying tips and beyond.

PACKABLE Nearly every recipe in this book has been developed to pack well. If I've shown it on a plate or in a bowl, you better believe that it can also go in a container. And I'm even giving you packing instructions to make sure the dish retains its maximum freshness, flavor, and texture.

MAKE-AHEAD If you want to win the lunch game, I cannot stress enough how essential meal prep is. Nearly every recipe in this book, or at least components from a recipe, can be made ahead. The packing tips (see Packable, above) are your guide to packing things quickly and properly for a lunch that tastes just as fresh on Friday as it does on Monday.

REHEAT You'll want to reheat most soups, stews, curries, and casseroles, so check for the reheat note at the top of the recipe if this is something you're looking for or looking to avoid. (Foods that require heating mean standing in a microwave line at work. Lucky for you, there are only a few of those kinds of recipes in this book.)

FREEZER-FRIENDLY If a recipe, or component of a recipe, can be frozen, you'll find this icon. Take comfort in knowing that these dishes will not have a compromised texture, taste, or appearance after defrosting.

LUNCH NOTES Read these if you're looking for recipe switch-ups to turn one meal into something seemingly brand-new, tips on turning a brunch feast into a workday lunch, ingredient swaps to make sure everyone at the table (or desk) is happy, and restyling notes to transform a container-packed lunch into a plated masterpiece with just a few swift moves.

DIETARY ICONS

Modern Lunch has recipes for all ways of eating, from omnivorous to fully vegan. Most meat, poultry, and fish recipes aren't integral to the dish; they're just a protein suggestion. On the opposite end of the spectrum, meat eaters can add, for example, chicken, beef, eggs, or cheese to vegan recipes. These recipes are flexible, so embrace your idea of the perfect lunch.

GLUTEN-FREE (GF) Includes no gluten-containing ingredients or grains.

VEGETARIAN (VG) Includes no meat, poultry, or fish but may include dairy or eggs.

VEGAN (V) Includes no meat, poultry, fish, eggs, or dairy.

PART I

LUNCH TO GO

(or to keep for here)

I'M A FIRM BELIEVER in taking a moment midday to feed yourself well, even if you eat at your desk, to make yourself and others (if you're sharing), feel special. A made-by-you packed lunch does this. It also saves time, energy, and money while bolstering you for the rest of the afternoon, regardless of what's thrown your way.

Homemade grab-and-go lunches, even for those of us who have the quickest commute in town (I work from home, for example), are convenient and help to streamline a day. And, for the most part, homemade packed lunches are healthier than their store-bought counterparts—and the recipes I'm sharing with you are no exception.

I personally find that if I don't prepare lunches or components for them ahead of time, I feel unprepared, grabbing this and that from the fridge, or I turn to less healthy takeout, or I just live on scrambled eggs. I've also watched my partner try to pack an unplanned lunch in the early morning before he heads out the door, and it always ends up as impulsive creations that he eventually brings back home and tosses in the trash. But if we take just an hour or two on the weekend to get ahead of the game, we can transform simple ingredients into meaningful, healthful, doable, and downright delicious lunches in a flash. An unexpected bonus of the modern lunch is that you get to sleep in a little longer as well as have a homemade meal ready to go for your workday—it's win-win.

In this section, you'll find meals and salads and meal-sized salads in jars that are visually alluring, scrumptious, practical—and you can literally throw one in your bag and head out the door. There are soups and stews that bring warmth to a chilly afternoon, making you feel comfortable in any surrounding. And, finally, lunch boxes that gather inspiration from the world into a focused, organized, and a genuinely enjoyable way to eat.

Note that nearly all of this book's recipes—not just the ones in this part—are fully packable (even the at-home and entertaining sections), so you can practice the packing skills you're learning here with almost any *Modern Lunch* recipe that speaks to you.

CHAPTER 1

Meals in Jars

IMAGINE THE DELIGHT of opening your bag to discover a gorgeously layered salad or robust, tossed grain bowl. These recipes can be prepared and stored days ahead, giving you a high-five every morning you open the refrigerator to get lunch together. Jar meals can be made in smaller portions, to act as sides that will complement whatever else you're packing for the day. Or, make them big, for tricked-out lunchtime creations that will sustain you all afternoon. Shake them and enjoy straight out of the jar, or transfer the insides to a serving bowl at work (I recommend IKEA for an under-$5 option).

I've found that having various proteins, lettuces, dressings, grains, cheeses, and vegetables—both raw and cooked—allows me to have a new lunch jar every day. No reruns, unless I want the same meal again, and often I do. Meal prepping at the start of the week will lead to endless possibilities.

9-Layer Salad

WITH LEMON CURRY DRESSING

In a way, the original 7-layer salad was the very first "meal in a jar," before meals in jars were popular. Nevertheless, the trifle-style assembly of yore is much fussier than I can imagine packing up for a modern weekday lunch, so I've simplified things, even though I've added 2 extra layers. I've chosen the vegetables here for their diverse yet complementary tastes, textures, and colors, and for their long-lasting physical structure—all important to make this meal multi-note, as opposed to one. But use any mixture of sweet/bitter/crispy/creamy produce you enjoy.

SERVES 4　⏳ 10 MINUTES　🕑 5 DAYS

LEMON CURRY DRESSING

½ cup lemon juice

½ cup unsweetened plain yogurt

¼ cup extra-virgin olive oil

1 Tbsp mild curry powder

½ tsp salt

¼ tsp minced garlic

Ground black pepper

SALAD

1 cup fresh shelled or frozen green peas

1 bulb fennel, cored, shaved or very thinly sliced

1 head radicchio, cored and shredded

2 carrots, shaved or grated

½ cup fresh herbs of choice (basil, parsley, mint)

4 cups baby arugula

1 cup shaved parmesan

4 servings protein of choice (see Lunch Note)

Lemon wedges

1　For the dressing, to a small bowl add the lemon juice, yogurt, olive oil, curry powder, salt, minced garlic, and pepper to taste, and whisk until fully combined. Store in an airtight container in the refrigerator until you are ready to assemble the salad jars.

2　To assemble the salad, divide dressing among 4 large jars. Top with the salad ingredients in the order listed. Seal and refrigerate, or take to go immediately.

3　Keep your jar chilled in the work refrigerator or with a cooler pack in your lunch bag. To serve, remove the lemon, shake up the jar, and then squeeze the lemon over top and enjoy. Or toss the salad in a serving bowl, season with the lemon, and then eat.

★ PICK YOUR PROTEIN

Protein keeps you fuller for longer, making it a must-have addition in my jar meals. Chicken, salmon, tuna, hard-boiled eggs, or canned white beans are what I reach for to bulk up this salad. Check out the Modern Meal Prep Staples chapter (page 235) for even more quick and easy lunchtime protein ideas.

Chicken and Cucumber Ribbon Salad

WITH PEANUT BUTTER VINAIGRETTE

Make-ahead cold foods, like the majority of recipes in this cookbook, need strong seasonings to wake everything up and taste as fresh and vibrant as the minute they were assembled. A punchy dressing made with peanut butter, a classic lunchtime staple, slicks a refreshing salad of mint, cucumber, green onions, chicken, and butter lettuce. This salad is the ultimate solution to those ho-hum cold, do-ahead meals you may be used to.

SERVES 4   ⏲ 10 MINUTES   ⏱ 5 DAYS

PEANUT BUTTER VINAIGRETTE

2 Tbsp lime juice

2 Tbsp natural peanut butter or favorite Nut Butter (page 237)

2 Tbsp tamari

1 Tbsp avocado oil or grapeseed oil

1 Tbsp maple syrup

1 Tbsp water

1 tsp fish sauce (optional)

¼ tsp red chili flakes

CHICKEN AND CUCUMBER RIBBON SALAD

Two 8 oz poached chicken breasts, shredded (page 239)

1 cup coarsely chopped fresh mint

3 green onions (white and green parts), sliced

1 English cucumber, peeled and sliced into ribbons with a vegetable peeler or cut into thin coins

2 heads butter lettuce or gem lettuce, leaves separated and torn

1 For the vinaigrette, in a small bowl, whisk the lime juice, peanut butter, tamari, oil, maple syrup, water, fish sauce (if using), and chili flakes until fully emulsified. If you are not using it immediately, store in an airtight glass jar for up to 1 week; just shake well before using.

2 For the salad, in a large bowl, combine the chicken, mint, and green onion. Keep the cucumber and lettuce separate for assembly.

3 To assemble, divide the dressing between 4 large jars. Add the chicken mixture on top of the dressing, followed by the cucumber and lettuce. Seal and refrigerate, or take to go immediately.

4 Keep chilled in the work refrigerator or with a cooler pack in your lunch bag. To serve, shake and enjoy directly out of the jar, or shake, transfer to a serving bowl, and eat.

★ **RESTYLE: STRETCH YOUR MEALS WITH QUINOA**
To lend a subtle nutty flavor, pleasing chewiness, and a little extra sauce-soaking power to this recipe, toss 1 cup of cooked quinoa (page 242) into the prepared chicken mixture. It also adds another serving to this recipe, so you can enjoy it the whole workweek.

Cold Noodle Salad

WITH SMOKED TOFU AND MISO-SESAME DRESSING

Prep, toss, pack, and go—that's it. This appetite-awakening recipe easily halves if there are fewer mouths to feed, though I find extras double as a nice no-cook dinner during the all-too-fleeting summer, maybe with a fried egg on top and Sriracha sauce polka-dotted on the edge of my bowl, giving the meal new life.

SERVES 4   ⏳ 15 MINUTES   ⏱ 4 DAYS

1   For the salad, bring a large pot of water to a boil; salt it well. Cook the spaghetti according to the package directions, drain, rinse with cold water, and drain again. Add the spaghetti to a large bowl along with the tofu, cabbage, bell pepper, mushrooms, cucumber, and cilantro.

2   For the dressing, in a medium bowl, whisk the lime juice, avocado oil or grapeseed oil, miso, tamari, sesame oil, ginger, and Sriracha to taste until fully combined. Add the dressing to the spaghetti mixture and toss gently to combine (clean hands work the best, I find).

3   To assemble, add the salad to 4 large jars, seal, and refrigerate or take to go immediately.

4   Once you arrive at work, keep your jar chilled in the refrigerator or with a cooler pack in your lunch bag. To serve, enjoy directly out of the jar or transfer to a serving bowl to eat.

★ **NOODLE NOTE**
Spaghetti made with wheat will stay tender longer than spaghetti made with brown rice flour (a gluten-free option), which can dry out with refrigeration. Both choices will still taste great, but the texture of leftovers suffers a little bit if you go the brown rice noodle route.

COLD NOODLE SALAD WITH SMOKED TOFU

Salt

8 oz (½ pound) regular spaghetti or brown rice spaghetti (see Lunch Note)

1 package (7½ oz) smoked tofu, cubed

3 cups finely sliced green or savoy cabbage

1 bell pepper, any color, seeded and thinly sliced

1 cup (about 6 whole) sliced cremini mushrooms

½ English cucumber, unpeeled and thinly sliced into rounds

¼ cup finely chopped fresh cilantro

MISO-SESAME DRESSING

3 Tbsp lime juice

2 Tbsp avocado oil or grapeseed oil

2 Tbsp white miso paste

2 Tbsp tamari

1 Tbsp toasted sesame oil

2 tsp grated fresh ginger or ½ tsp ground dried ginger

Sriracha

Quick and Easy Salad Inspirations

I love salad any time of year, and truly believe that the modern salad, one that can incorporate lettuce but doesn't have to, is the perfect lunch to go. And the same ingredients with tweaked proportions and a different dressing can transform into something brand-new tomorrow. Big flavor, awesome texture, and portability are key to a take-along salad, whether packed in a jar or other container. Some of these recipes require a bit of meal prep, which is the foundation for a successful modern lunch, but many can be assembled in a couple of minutes before you dash out the door.

JAR SALAD PRINCIPLES Dressing on the bottom, ingredients layered from heaviest to lightest. Season with salt and pepper, to taste.

CONTAINER SALAD PRINCIPLES Dressing packed on the side, ingredients tossed or layered from heaviest to lightest.

10 Salads Using Meal Prep Staples

SALAD baby arugula + cubed roasted sweet potatoes + diced celery + cubed roasted chicken + grated parmesan
DRESSING Balsamic Vinaigrette (page 236)

SALAD boiled baby new potatoes + shredded radicchio + sliced grilled steak + orange segments
DRESSING Green Goddess Dressing (page 237)

SALAD shredded romaine + halved cherry tomatoes + chopped bacon + cubed roasted chicken
DRESSING Creamy Caesar Dressing (page 236)

SALAD rehydrated rice vermicelli noodles + prepared kimchi + chopped steamed broccoli + cubed smoked tofu + toasted cashews
DRESSING Sesame Orange Vinaigrette (page 237)

SALAD cooked brown rice + cooked ground beef + diced cucumber + pomegranate seeds + chopped fresh mint
DRESSING yogurt + olive oil + lemon juice + za'atar

SALAD spring mix lettuce + cubed roasted squash + hard-boiled eggs + toasted pumpkin seeds + thinly sliced apple + grated aged cheddar
DRESSING Balsamic Vinaigrette (page 236)

SALAD rehydrated couscous + cubed roasted parsnips + baby spinach + canned chickpeas + chopped walnuts + raisins
DRESSING Tahini-Yogurt Dressing (page 237)

SALAD sliced grilled halloumi + chopped romaine + cooked quinoa + sliced peaches + chopped fresh parsley
DRESSING canned coconut milk + chili jam + lime juice + tamari

SALAD sliced roasted eggplant + sliced roasted zucchini + sliced roasted onions + cubed roasted chicken + crumbled feta
DRESSING olive oil + balsamic vinegar + minced red Thai chilis

SALAD cooked penne + sliced grilled steak + baby arugula + grated parmesan + chopped toasted walnuts
DRESSING olive oil + prepared sun-dried tomato pesto + lemon juice

10 Salads You Can Make in a Pinch

SALAD baby spinach + marinated artichoke quarters + canned tuna + canned white beans + halved cherry tomatoes
DRESSING lemon juice + olive oil + Dijon mustard

SALAD shredded romaine + grated carrots + diced cucumber + chopped cilantro + flaked hot-smoked trout + crumbled prepared papadums
DRESSING mango chutney + yogurt + lemon juice + curry powder

SALAD canned lentils + diced vacuum-packed pre-cooked beets + chopped radicchio + chopped roasted almonds
DRESSING olive oil + balsamic vinegar + diced chili

SALAD spiralized zucchini noodles + cooked corn kernels + canned tuna + halved cherry tomatoes + minced green onion
DRESSING mayonnaise + lemon juice

SALAD variety of sliced tomatoes + fresh mozzarella + toasted sunflower seeds + diced salami
DRESSING olive oil + sherry vinegar + smoked paprika + salt

SALAD cubed cantaloupe + thinly sliced radishes + prosciutto + sliced jarred roasted red peppers
DRESSING Greek yogurt + olive oil + lime juice

SALAD spring mix lettuce + sliced peaches + shaved fennel + crumbled goat cheese + capocollo + sliced red onion
DRESSING olive oil + balsamic vinegar

SALAD chopped iceberg lettuce + diced organic deli turkey + cubed cheddar + cubed cucumber + halved cherry tomatoes
DRESSING mayonnaise + buttermilk + lemon juice + ground black pepper

SALAD canned lentils + sliced pears + spring mix lettuce + blue cheese + toasted chopped walnuts
DRESSING olive oil + apple cider vinegar + Dijon mustard

SALAD canned black beans + shredded romaine + prepared corn salsa + cubed avocado + crumbled feta + tortilla chips
DRESSING olive oil + lime juice

Chicken, Celery, and Apple Waldorf

WITH OAT GROATS

This is good, simple, family-friendly lunchtime food. Little ones enjoy this salad's pleasing mildness, while adults gravitate toward its ease of preparation, comfort food appeal, and real-food ingredient list. Oat groats offer a gluten-free option but barley (quicker cooking but not gluten-free) will give the same chewy, substantial quality to this one-bowl, one-jar meal.

SERVES 4 ⧖ 10 MINUTES ⏱ 3 DAYS

1   For the salad, to a large bowl, add the oats or barley, chicken, celery, and apples and mix well to combine.

2   For the dressing, to a small bowl, add the mayonnaise, lemon juice, garlic, dill, salt, and pepper to taste and whisk to combine.

3   To assemble, add the dressing to the salad and mix until fully combined. Add the dressed salad to 4 large jars and top with the lettuce. Seal and refrigerate, or take to go immediately.

4   If you are taking this jar to work, keep it in the refrigerator or tucked away with a cooler pack in your lunch bag. To serve, shake and enjoy it directly out of the jar, or shake it and then transfer to a serving bowl to enjoy.

★ **RESTYLE: MAKE IT TO-STAY**
Skip the spring mix lettuce and add the salad to Bibb lettuce cups. Garnish with halved seedless grapes and sprinkle with toasted chopped walnuts.

CHICKEN, CELERY, AND APPLE WALDORF SALAD

4 cups cooked oat groats (page 242) or barley (page 241)

Four 4 oz roasted or poached chicken breasts (page 239), cooled and diced

4 stalks celery, diced

2 apples, diced

4 cups packed spring mix lettuce

CREAMY LEMON-DILL DRESSING

½ cup mayonnaise

¼ cup lemon juice

½ clove garlic, minced

1 Tbsp finely chopped fresh dill or 1 tsp dried dill

¾ tsp salt

Ground black pepper

Sweet Potato Noodle Salad

WITH CHICKEN AND TAMARIND DRESSING

Sweet potatoes are sturdy and absorbent, two qualities that make them work beautifully as the base in this sweet-and-sour salad. The dressing is laced with naturally acidic and caramel-like tamarind, which I'm able to find in my regular grocery store pressed into a brick, but if you can't, it's readily available online now, too. If you can't find tamarind anywhere, substitute finely chopped soft, pitted dried dates to provide the sweetness of tamarind in the dressing.

SERVES 4   ⌛ 20 MINUTES   ⏱ 3 DAYS

SWEET POTATO NOODLE SALAD

Two 4 oz boneless, skinless chicken breasts

2 sweet potatoes, peeled and spiral sliced into thin noodles or shredded

4 cups baby greens of choice (arugula, kale, spinach, etc.)

1 cup fresh Thai or regular basil leaves, finely chopped

2 green onions (white and green parts), finely chopped

TAMARIND DRESSING

1 tsp lime zest

3 Tbsp lime juice

2 Tbsp avocado oil or olive oil (not extra-virgin)

2 Tbsp tamari

1 Tbsp tamarind paste, finely chopped to remove any large pieces

1 tsp fish sauce (optional)

Sriracha

1   For the salad, bring a large pot of water to a boil, salt well, and reduce to a very gentle simmer at the lowest heat. Add the chicken and poach until it is tender and cooked through (do not boil rapidly or the chicken will toughen), 10 to 12 minutes. The thickest part of the chicken should read 160°F to 165°F on a meat thermometer. Pull the chicken out of the water using tongs (do not discard the water), and rest it for 5 minutes before shredding it. Place the chicken in a large bowl.

2   Return the reserved poaching liquid to a boil, and blanch the sweet potato noodles for 30 seconds to 1 minute maximum (any longer and they'll fall apart), just to take the raw edge off. Drain well and add to the shredded chicken. Let cool for 10 minutes.

3   For the dressing, in a small bowl or mini food processor, whisk or blend the lime zest and juice, oil, tamari, tamarind, fish sauce (if using), and Sriracha to taste. If you are whisking by hand, try to blend the tamarind into the liquid as best you can; it's okay if it's not perfectly smooth.

4   To assemble, add the dressing to the sweet potato noodles and chicken, along with baby greens, basil, and green onion. Gently mix with clean hands and divide among 4 large jars. Seal and refrigerate, or take to go immediately.

5   When you arrive at work, keep your jar chilled in the refrigerator or with a cooler pack in your lunch bag. To serve, shake and enjoy in the jar, or shake and transfer to a serving bowl to eat.

Instant Warm Moroccan Couscous Salad

⅓ cup couscous

¼ cup cooked chickpeas, drained, rinsed if using canned

¼ cup grated carrot

4 grape or cherry tomatoes, halved

2–4 green olives, pitted and sliced (optional)

2 tsp dried currants or raisins

2 Tbsp chopped fresh parsley

1 Tbsp extra-virgin olive oil

1 Tbsp orange juice or orange marmalade

2 tsp harissa paste or curry paste of choice

¼ tsp ground cumin

¼ tsp salt

1 lemon wedge

2 Tbsp toasted sliced almonds

½ cup just-boiled water from the kettle

This jar meal takes help from the kettle for rehydrating and heating, for a dish that pretty much "cooks" itself. Even if your workplace is a coffee shop, which mine sometimes is, you'll have access to the piping hot water required to make this recipe. I like to switch up the add-ins with combinations like roasted vegetables and chopped chicken, marinara sauce and white beans, and black beans and cooked sweet potato. Because couscous will take on any flavor it's given in this quick and easy recipe, the possibilities are endless. For a delicious topping, pack a ziplock baggie full of garnishes like crumbled feta or crumbled bacon to add to the salad once it's rehydrated and warmed through.

SERVES 1   ⧖ 12 MINUTES   ⊕ 3 DAYS

1   For the salad, to a large jar or heatproof container, add the couscous, chickpeas, carrot, tomatoes, green olives (if using), currants, parsley, oil, orange juice or marmalade, harissa or curry paste, cumin, and salt. Add the lemon wedge on top, and a small baggie containing the almonds, and a small baggie containing the almonds, seal, and refrigerate until you are ready to use it.

2   To serve, remove the lemon wedge and pour ½ cup of just-boiled water from the kettle into the jar, seal, and set aside to warm and rehydrate for 5 to 7 minutes, until the couscous has absorbed all of the water and is fluffy. Season with a squeeze of lemon, stir well with a fork to combine, top with almonds, and enjoy.

Springtime Pasta Salad

WITH TUNA AND CREAMY PESTO DRESSING

Crisp, creamy, and vibrant springtime ingredients come together in this jarred, saladized homage to tuna casserole. Keeping the dressing on the bottom until serving keeps this salad tasting fresher for longer—these noodles have a tendency to dry out if they sit in their dressing for too long. I favor a sparing addition of protein-rich quinoa pasta, leaving you with energy for the afternoon—as opposed to leaving you primed for a 3:00 p.m. desk nap.

SERVES 4   ⧗ 15 MINUTES   ⊕ 4 DAYS

1   For the pasta salad, bring a medium saucepan full of water to a boil; salt well. Cook the pasta according to the package directions, adding the asparagus and peas to blanch in the last minute of cooking time. Drain the pot and rinse with cold water, and then drain again. Transfer the pasta mixture to a large bowl and add the celery, onion, lemon zest, and salt. Toss until combined.

2   For the dressing, to a small bowl, add the lemon juice, mayonnaise, pesto, mustard, and pepper to taste, and whisk to combine.

3   To assemble, to 4 large jars, add the dressing followed by the tuna and the pasta mixture. Seal and refrigerate, or take to go immediately.

4   Keep in your work refrigerator or stored in your lunch bag with a cooler pack. To serve, shake and enjoy directly out of the jar or shake, and then transfer to a serving bowl to enjoy.

SPRINGTIME PASTA SALAD

4 oz small quinoa pasta or small whole-grain pasta

½ lb asparagus, tough ends removed, cut into 1-inch pieces

½ cup fresh shelled or frozen green peas

2 stalks celery, finely sliced

¼ cup minced white onion

1 tsp lemon zest

¼ tsp salt

Two 6 oz cans (or 4 mini cans) solid tuna in olive oil, drained and coarsely flaked

CREAMY PESTO DRESSING

2 Tbsp lemon juice

2 Tbsp mayonnaise

2 Tbsp green pesto, homemade (see No-Recipe Green Pesto, page 68) or prepared

1 Tbsp Dijon mustard

Ground black pepper

French Lentil Salad

WITH ROASTED RADISHES, PEAS, AND EGGS

Nice, France, the birthplace of *salade Niçoise*, is where I learned that this dish is a balance of quiet colors, delicate textures, and loud flavors. Layering for a to-go lunch means you can practice the French art of *pique-nique* wherever you may find yourself.

SERVES 4   ⏳ 30 MINUTES   🕐 4 DAYS

1   For the salad, preheat the oven to 375°F. On a large rimmed baking sheet, toss the radishes with the oil and salt to taste. Roast for 20 to 25 minutes, until the radishes are tender and lightly browned on the bottom.

2   In a large bowl, toss the roasted radishes, lentils, peas, olives, and vinaigrette until combined.

3   To assemble, add a serving of the lentil mixture to each of 4 large jars, and top with the lettuce and eggs. Seal and refrigerate, or take to go immediately.

4   Store in the work refrigerator or with a cooler pack in your lunch bag. To serve, without shaking, enjoy it directly out of the jar, or transfer it to a serving bowl. If eating at home, line a plate of a bowl with lettuce, top with the lentil salad and egg, then enjoy.

★ **BOOST TOMORROW'S SALAD**
To perk up the lentil salad, add a dash of additional vinaigrette or lemon juice before serving. This trick is especially helpful after the salad has been assembled for a few days, and also works for any other recipe with beans or legumes.

8 radishes, quartered

1 Tbsp extra-virgin olive oil

Salt

2 cups cooked brown or French lentils, well drained

1 cup fresh shelled or frozen green peas

15 Niçoise or kalamata olives, pitted and chopped

½ cup (8 Tbsp) French Vinaigrette (page 236)

4 cups lettuce of choice, such as baby gem, baby spinach, or red leaf, torn if necessary

4–8 hard-boiled eggs, peeled, halved (page 238)

Cauliflower Fatteh

WITH PINE NUTS AND DATES

Fatteh is a Levantine dish combining flatbread or pita with chickpeas and a silky yogurt tahini sauce. I followed less traditional guidelines and wove in my own lunchtime take on the dish with cauliflower and dates, making it feel more like a vegetable-forward salad. It's dynamic, changing in texture and taste with each passing minute.

SERVES 4   ⧗ 20 MINUTES   ⏱ 3 DAYS

CAULIFLOWER FATTEH

2 Tbsp extra-virgin olive oil

½ head cauliflower, cored, florets thinly sliced

One 19 oz can chickpeas, drained and rinsed or 2 cups cooked chickpeas

6 dates, pitted and chopped

¼ cup pine nuts

1 tsp ground cumin

1 tsp salt

Red chili flakes

2 Tbsp finely chopped mint

4 small pitas or lavash breads, toasted until very crisp, torn

YOGURT TAHINI SAUCE

½ cup plain whole-milk yogurt

¼ cup tahini

6 Tbsp lemon juice

2 tsp maple syrup

¼ tsp salt

1   For the fatteh, in a large high-sided skillet or cast-iron pan, heat the oil over medium-high heat until shimmering. Add the cauliflower and let it cook for 2 minutes without stirring to begin browning. Stir and cook until the florets are golden brown in a few places and tender, 5 to 8 minutes longer. Stir in the chickpeas, dates, pine nuts, cumin, salt, and chili flakes to taste. Sauté for 2 to 3 minutes longer, until the mixture is melded and warm. Remove from the heat, stir in the mint, and allow to cool slightly.

2   For the sauce, in a medium bowl, whisk all the sauce ingredients until fully combined.

3   To assemble, to 4 large jars, add the cauliflower mixture and spoon the sauce over top. Top the contents of each jar with crumbled pita or lavash. Seal and refrigerate, or take to go immediately.

4   At work, keep your meal chilled in the refrigerator or store it with a cooler pack in your lunch bag. To serve, shake or mix with a fork and enjoy directly out of the jar or from a serving bowl.

CHAPTER 2

Soups and Stews

THE RECIPES IN this chapter will warm and welcome you to the afternoon; nutritionally fortifying soups, stews, and other warming delights offer soothing sustenance at lunch. And while warm soups have a reputation as cold-weather staples, I happily eat them all year long, especially if I'm feeling a bit rough around the edges.

You'll find the "instant" noodles in this chapter tinged with nostalgia but made fresher, healthier, and more flavorful, and the other soups and stews satisfy on all levels, with lean protein, sometimes grains, a whack of vegetables, and assertive seasonings. Reheat them until almost boiling on the stove and pack in a preheated thermal container. Or pack them up cold and reheat them at work.

Just-Add-Water Miso, Sweet Potato, and Soba Ramen

The natural sweetness and creaminess of sweet potato helps to create a ramen broth that's both addictive and nourishing. Soba noodles, made from buckwheat flour (check the label for 100 percent buckwheat flour to make sure they're gluten-free, if that's a priority), offer a nutty quality to the dish while mushrooms and the requisite soft-boiled jammy egg give a familiar umami tang. Greens are required here, for me at least, making this healthy meal-in-a-jar (or container or bowl) look and feel three-dimensional. The just-add-water method means no accidental spills and a lighter lunch to take in your bag.

SERVES 4   ⧗ 30 MINUTES   ⧖ 1 WEEK FOR MISO SWEET POTATO BROTH CONCENTRATE; 5 DAYS ASSEMBLED

1   For the broth concentrate, steam the sweet potato until tender, about 10 minutes. Add to a blender or food processor along with 1 cup water, bouillon powder, miso paste, rice vinegar, ginger, sesame oil, and Sriracha to taste, and then blend until smooth. Transfer the mixture to a jar and store in an airtight container in the refrigerator for up to 1 week.

2   For the vegetables, eggs, and soba noodles, preheat the oven to 425°F and bring a large pot of water to a boil.

3   Toss the mushrooms with the sesame oil and tamari. Place the mushrooms on a large rimmed baking sheet and roast for 15 minutes, until shrunken and deep brown. Set aside.

4   Carefully place the eggs in boiling water and cook for 6 minutes. Fill a medium bowl with cold water. Once the 6 minutes are up, use a slotted spoon to remove the eggs from the pot and place them in the bowl of cold water to help loosen the shell, keeping the boiling water on the stove for the noodles. Gently peel the eggs, being careful not to break the white or the yolk will run out

CONTINUED

RAMEN BROTH CONCENTRATE

1 small or ½ large (7 oz) sweet potato, peeled and chunked

1 cup water, plus more for steaming sweet potato

2 Tbsp organic vegetable or chicken bouillon powder

2 Tbsp white miso paste

1 Tbsp rice vinegar

2 tsp minced fresh ginger

¼ tsp toasted sesame oil

Sriracha

VEGETABLES, EGGS, AND SOBA NOODLES

4 portobello mushrooms, diced

1 Tbsp toasted sesame oil

1 Tbsp gluten-free tamari

4 large eggs

2 bundles (6½ oz) soba noodles (buckwheat noodles)

2 cups steamed greens (broccoli, broccoli rabe, kale, etc.) or packed raw spinach

Black sesame seeds (optional)

Minced fresh red Thai chili (optional)

4 cups (1 cup per serving) just-boiled water from the kettle, for serving

(they're not as sturdy as hard-boiled eggs), and set aside. Then, cook the noodles in the reserved boiling water according to package directions, until tender. Drain the noodles, rinse with cold water, drain again, and set aside.

5   To assemble, for each serving, add ½ cup of broth concentrate to a large jar or airtight container or build at home in a bowl. Top the broth with a portion each of noodles, mushrooms, steamed greens or spinach, a peeled whole egg, and sesame seeds and chili to taste. Seal and store refrigerated.

6   When you're ready for lunch, for each serving, pour 1 cup (enough to cover) of boiling water over top, seal, and let stand for 3 minutes to reheat fully. Open the lid, give the soup a gentle stir, slice the egg in half with your spoon, and then eat.

∗ GO PLANT-BASED

To make this meal vegan, use vegetable bouillon and replace the egg with cubed smoked tofu.

Harissa, Squash, and Chickpea Stew

WITH KALE CHIPS

The tension between sweet orange and smoky-spicy harissa pulls you in a different direction with each spoonful of this soup. The kale chips are a tasty snack on their own, but if you do stir them in after baking, although they go soft, they retain their faux deep-fried flavor. It's ridiculously good, worth sacrificing at least half the batch of crispy chips for.

SERVES 4   ⧖ 20 MINUTES   ⧗ 5 DAYS

1   For the kale chips, preheat the oven to 425°F.

2   On a large rimmed baking sheet, massage the kale with oil and salt to taste. Spread in a single layer (they need room or they won't crisp). Roast for 15 to 20 minutes, tossing every 5 minutes, or until all the chips are fully crisped. Turn off the oven and leave the kale chips in the oven with the door ajar for up to 15 minutes (this step is optional, but it does ensure the chips are very dry, if making ahead). Store kale chips at room temperature, loosely covered, for 4 to 5 days.

3   For the stew, in a large pot, heat the oil and harissa over medium heat. Once fragrant, add the squash, onion, and garlic and sauté for 8 minutes. Add the chickpeas, water, orange juice, and salt. Bring to a boil, reduce to a simmer, cover and cook for 15 minutes, until the squash is creamy and tender. Stir once or twice, adding more water if a thinner consistency is desired (the stew thickens upon cooling).

CONTINUED

KALE CHIPS

½ bunch (4 cups) curly kale, de-stemmed and torn

1 tsp extra-virgin olive oil

Salt

HARISSA, SQUASH, AND CHICKPEA STEW

2 Tbsp extra-virgin olive oil or coconut oil

1–3 Tbsp DIY Harissa Paste or prepared harissa paste (see Lunch Notes)

One 2–3 lb creamy-fleshed squash like red kuri or buttercup (butternut is too stringy here), seeded, peeled, and cut into 1-inch cubes

1 onion, diced

1 clove garlic, minced

2 cups cooked chickpeas

2 cups water

½ cup orange juice

½ tsp salt

4   If eating immediately, ladle the hot stew into bowls, garnish with kale chips, and enjoy. If packing to go, add the stew to a container or preheated thermal container, and pack kale chips on the side in a separate small container or ziplock baggie. To serve, reheat the stew, if necessary, garnish with kale chips or serve them on the side, and enjoy.

★ **HEAT LEVELS: PREPARED HARISSA VS. HOMEMADE HARISSA**
Store-bought harissa paste can be quite spicy, making the full 3 tablespoons this recipe calls for too much for some tastes. If you are using the homemade harissa paste (recipe below), you can get away with the full 3 tablespoons without it being overly spicy—though it will still have some bite.

★ **DIY HARISSA PASTE**
In a food processor, pulse 2 cloves of garlic until minced. Add ¼ cup of extra-virgin olive oil, one 5.5-ounce can of tomato paste, 1 tablespoon of lemon juice, 1 tablespoon of red chili flakes, 1 tablespoon of smoked paprika, 2 teaspoons of caraway seeds, and 2 teaspoons of ground cumin; process until smooth. Store in an airtight container in the refrigerator for up to 2 weeks or freeze in ¼ cup portions for up to 2 months.

Tomato Sourdough Soup

WITH CACIO E PEPE SOCCA TRIANGLES

While I've been to Tuscany, I sadly didn't try *pappa al pomodoro*, the famed tomato bread soup on location. Regardless, this hasn't stopped me from trying to recreate it at home. Tomato soup and a sandwich are lunchtime classics that I ate hundreds of times in my youth. Here, they're made more substantial and "adult" with crisp-on-the-outside, chewy-on-the-inside socca (chickpea flour) triangles modeled after *cacio e pepe* (cheese and pepper) pasta.

SERVES 4 TO 6 · 25 MINUTES · 5 DAYS FOR TOMATO SOURDOUGH SOUP; 1 DAY FOR CACIO E PEPE SOCCA TRIANGLES

TOMATO SOURDOUGH SOUP

- 2 Tbsp extra-virgin olive oil
- 1 onion, finely chopped
- 2 cloves garlic, minced
- 1 tsp Italian seasoning or ½ tsp dried oregano + ½ tsp dried basil
- ½ tsp salt
- Ground black pepper
- One 28 oz can whole tomatoes
- 2 cups rustic sourdough bread (ends are best), cubed
- 3 cups water
- 1 tsp red wine vinegar

CACIO E PEPE SOCCA TRIANGLES

- 1 cup chickpea flour
- 1 cup water
- ½ cup finely grated parmesan cheese
- ¼ tsp salt
- ¼ tsp coarsely ground black pepper

1. For the soup, in a large pot, heat the oil over medium heat. Add the onion, garlic, Italian seasoning, salt, and pepper to taste. Sauté for 8 to 10 minutes, until the onions are translucent. Add the tomatoes, bread, water, and vinegar. Bring to a boil, reduce to a simmer, cover, and cook for 15 minutes. Remove from the heat and pulse with an immersion blender until mostly smooth (leave a little texture).
2. For the socca, preheat the oven to 350°F. Line a standard loaf pan with parchment paper. In a medium bowl, combine the chickpea flour, water, parmesan, salt, and pepper. Bake for 10 to 12 minutes, or until dry on top and starting to crack. Leave the oven on. Cool in the pan for 10 minutes, and then remove and slice crosswise into 4 rectangles, and then slice each rectangle in half diagonally for 8 triangles (or make them any dip-worthy shape you choose). Place on a parchment-lined baking sheet, leaving room between the triangles. Bake for 5 minutes longer, or until the edges are dry.
3. If eating immediately, heat the soup until piping hot, ladle into bowls, season with additional pepper, and serve alongside the socca. If you are packing to go, ladle the soup into a container or a preheated thermal container. Pack the socca separately wrapped in plastic or foil. Reheat the soup, if necessary, and serve with socca for dipping.

★ SAVE THAT DOUGH

Farmers' markets will often sell day-old bread at very low prices. I've managed to score a few $2 day-old loaves that go for $6 fresh. It works perfectly well in this recipe, if not better.

Savory Vegetable Cobbler

This lunch is served family-style, with individual whole-grain biscuits to make it personal. It's a healthy take on cold-weather comfort food, allowing you to get back to your day without drifting into a food-induced nap—though sometimes that's nice in the dead of winter.

SERVES 4   ⧖ 1 HOUR   ⏲ 4 DAYS

1   Preheat the oven to 350°F.

2   For the filling, in a large pot, heat the butter over medium heat until foamy. Add the celery, potatoes, squash, onion, carrots, and garlic. Season with, salt, pepper, and nutmeg. Sauté for 10 minutes, until the onions are translucent and the vegetables have begun to soften. Stir in the flour and cook for 1 minute, until nutty in fragrance, and then add the chickpeas. Slowly stir in the broth, milk, and lemon juice. Bring to a boil, reduce to a simmer, and cook uncovered for 15 minutes, stirring often. Using an immersion blender or potato masher, pulse or mash the mixture to thicken it without pureeing it completely (just a few pulses are sufficient). Stir in the parsley. Transfer the mixture to a large cast-iron skillet or glass or ceramic 9- × 13-inch baking dish. Set aside.

3   For the biscuits, in a large bowl, combine the flour, cornmeal, baking powder, and salt. Cut in the butter using your fingers until fully incorporated. Using a spoon, stir in the water or milk until a pliable dough that holds together forms. Gather the dough into a round, flour the counter lightly, and roll to ½ inch in thickness. Cut into 6 to 8 (3-inch) biscuit rounds, rerolling as needed. Place the biscuits on top of the cobbler, spacing evenly.

4   Bake for 35 to 45 minutes, until the filling is bubbling and the biscuits are dry to the touch. If freezing, once baked, cool completely and then wrap tightly and freeze up to 2 months.

5   If serving immediately, spoon the hot cobbler into bowls and enjoy. If packing to go, spoon into containers, cool, seal, and refrigerate until you are ready to use it. To serve, reheat before eating.

FILLING

2 Tbsp unsalted butter or vegan butter

4 stalks celery, cut into medium pieces

2 Yukon Gold potatoes, cut into medium pieces

Half a 2 lb kabocha or butternut squash, seeded, peeled, and cut into medium pieces

1 onion, cut into medium pieces

1 large carrot, cut into medium rounds

2 cloves garlic, minced

½ tsp salt

Ground black pepper

¼ tsp grated nutmeg

2 Tbsp light spelt flour

One 19 oz can chickpeas, drained and rinsed

2 cups low-sodium vegetable broth

1 cup whole milk or unsweetened plain almond milk

1 Tbsp lemon juice

¼ cup finely chopped fresh parsley

BISCUITS

1 cup light spelt flour

½ cup cornmeal

2 tsp baking powder

½ tsp salt

2 Tbsp unsalted butter (room temperature or cold)

½ cup water or whole milk or unsweetened plain almond milk

Spanish Lentils

WITH OLIVES, ALMONDS, AND SAFFRON

In Spain, I admired that everywhere from pinxtos bars to fine dining restaurants made fruity Spanish olive oil and fragrant sherry vinegar available on the bar top or table for seasoning in a similar style to salt and pepper shakers. The two condiments, especially the vinegar, really made savory food pop. Here, I've used sherry vinegar to brighten an earthy pot of lentils, olives, and carrots infused with saffron. If it's summertime and just too hot to think about a bubbling pot of lentil stew for lunch, serve the dish just-warm, at room temperature, or chilled, blanketing a piece of grilled bread (soaked in olive oil, if you please) for an afternoon treat on the weekend (see the Lunch Note for the how-to).

SERVES 5   ⧗ 45 MINUTES   ⟳ 1 WEEK

1. If using raw lentils, in a medium saucepan, add the lentils and cover with 4 inches of water. Bring to a boil, reduce the heat to medium-low, and cook until tender, 20 to 25 minutes. Drain and rinse with cold water. While the lentils are cooking, begin the stew.

2. In a large high-sided skillet or Dutch oven, heat the oil over medium heat. Add the onion, carrots, and garlic and sauté for 8 to 10 minutes, until the onions are translucent and the carrots are beginning to get tender. Add the tomatoes and break up large pieces with a spoon. Stir in the vinegar, olives, saffron, and chili flakes to taste, bring to a boil, reduce to a simmer, cover, and cook for 15 to 20 minutes. Stir in the basil. If freezing, omit the basil, transfer the lentil mixture to an airtight container, and freeze up to 3 months. Stir in the basil when reheating.

3. If you are using raw almonds, toast them in a dry skillet over low heat for 8 to 10 minutes, or until they are fragrant and beginning to brown.

CONTINUED

1 cup uncooked brown lentils or 2½ cups cooked brown lentils

2 Tbsp extra-virgin olive oil

1 onion, diced

2 carrots, cut into thin rounds

2 cloves garlic, slivered

one 28 oz can whole tomatoes

2 Tbsp sherry vinegar

8 manzanilla (Spanish green) olives, pitted and quartered

¼ tsp saffron threads

Red chili flakes

¼ cup sliced fresh basil, plus more for serving

½ cup chopped raw or roasted almonds

4   To serve, if eating immediately, ladle the stew into bowls and top with some basil and the almonds. If packing to go, ladle the stew into a container or a preheated thermal container. Pack the extra basil and the almonds in a separate container or small ziplock baggie. Reheat the stew if necessary, garnish with almonds, and eat.

★ ON TOAST

To amplify lunchtime on the weekend, take thickly sliced grilled or toasted rustic bread, rub with a halved garlic clove, generously drizzle with olive oil, and top with this stew. Spanish manchego cheese shaved over top to finish would not be overkill.

Broccoli, Rigatoni, and White Bean Minestrone

WITH FRIED LEMONS

Elegant, quick, and easy to keep going back to for another ladleful, this soup changes as the days go by. Fresh from the pot, the broth is creamy and vibrant; as it sits, the noodles, broccoli, and beans soak the liquid gold up almost entirely, turning this into a hearty stew. The fried lemon slices add a gently bitter-sour-sweet-charred pop of sunshine to the top of each bowl.

SERVES 6 ⧗ 25 MINUTES ⟳ 5 DAYS (SEE LUNCH NOTE)

1 For the minestrone, in a large pot, heat the olive oil over medium heat. Add the onion, garlic, broccoli stems, thyme, and salt, and season with pepper. Sauté until the onions are translucent, 8 to 10 minutes.

2 Add the broth, water, and parmesan rind (if using), and bring to a boil. Add the pasta and beans. Return to a boil, reduce the heat to medium-low, and cook for 8 minutes, until the pasta is cooked al dente. Add the broccoli florets and lemon juice and cook until the broccoli is tender, about 3 minutes. Remove the parmesan rind and season the soup with additional salt to taste.

3 For the fried lemons, fill a medium saucepan halfway with water and bring to a boil. Cut the lemons into very thin slices, discarding any seeds. Add to the boiling water and blanch for 3 minutes. Drain well.

4 In a medium cast-iron or nonstick skillet, heat the avocado oil over medium-high heat. Add the lemon slices in a single layer and fry them until golden brown on the bottom side, 4 to 5 minutes. Flip and fry for another minute on the second side, until brown. Transfer to a plate.

CONTINUED

BROCCOLI, RIGATONI, AND WHITE BEAN MINESTRONE

2 Tbsp extra-virgin olive oil

1 onion, diced

2 cloves garlic, thinly sliced

1 head broccoli, stem peeled and sliced, top cut into florets

1 tsp dried thyme

½ tsp salt

Ground black pepper

4 cups vegetable broth

2 cups water

3-inch piece parmesan rind (optional, if you have one stashed away in your freezer)

4 oz rigatoni (see Lunch Note)

One 19 oz can white beans, drained and rinsed

1 Tbsp lemon juice

FRIED LEMONS

2 whole lemons, preferably organic, scrubbed

2 Tbsp avocado oil or olive oil (not extra-virgin)

5   To serve, if eating immediately, ladle the soup into bowls and garnish with the fried lemons. If packing to go, ladle the soup into a container and pack the fried lemons on the side. Reheat the soup, garnish with fried lemons, and enjoy.

★ **MAKE-AHEAD: AVOID OVERCOOKED NOODLES**
If you are making this recipe in advance, prepare it without the pasta, adding the noodles to cook only on reheating. Or replace the noodles altogether with a hardier grain that can withstand the test of time and another heating, like barley, farro, oat groats, or wheat berries. If you don't mind extra-soft noodles (to be honest, sometimes I find comfort in that texture), disregard this tip and cook the recipe as written.

CHAPTER 3

Contemporary Lunch Boxes

IF YOU HAVEN'T JOINED the meal prep movement (or if you have but prefer to call it something different because the term sounds grossly unhip), the lunch boxes in this chapter are a dream come true. They're made to be versatile, too, so I've supplied a few of my favorite no-recipe recipe combos (based on your dietary requirements), to flow throughout the seasons.

And I'm using the term "lunch box" loosely. Any gear you have, be it a locking glass container, divided bento box, or stainless steel tiffin tin, can transport your lunch in a way that keeps food fresher for longer, packs cleanly, and can be taken anywhere you require a meal on the run. To work, on the road, on a plane, a train, a picnic table, a campground, even at home, if you like.

These are adult-appropriate, full-meal lunch boxes that don't feel dinky or juvenile (but if you have an adventurous little eater in the house, smaller portions can work for them, too). They're nutritionally boosted with make-ahead vegetables, proteins, and palate-awakening seasonings.

Divide and conquer lunchtime hunger.

Asparagus and Pea Pilaf

WITH EGGS AND MOZZARELLA

1½ cups water

½ cup basmati rice

½ cup quinoa

½ lb asparagus, tough ends trimmed, cut into ½-inch pieces

1 cup fresh shelled or frozen green peas

½ tsp lemon zest

3 Tbsp lemon juice, plus lemon wedges for serving

2 Tbsp extra-virgin olive oil

¼ cup pitted, diced kalamata olives

1 Tbsp finely chopped fresh dill

1 Tbsp finely chopped fresh mint

½ tsp salt

Ground black pepper

4–6 oz fresh mozzarella, coarsely torn or cubed into small pieces

4 hard-boiled eggs, peeled and halved, or cubes of avocado tossed in lemon juice

While there's nothing greater than the abundance of produce available in the summer, springtime produce—especially the greens—take me by surprise each year after a winter of hearty root vegetables. This lunchbox is fresh and light, filling you with the sunny flavors of warmer days to come. Make this year-round with perennially available broccoli instead of asparagus, and frozen peas in place of fresh.

SERVES 4   ⏳ 30 MINUTES   ⏱ 4 DAYS

1   For the salad, in a medium saucepan, bring the water, rice, and quinoa to a boil, reduce to a simmer, cover, and cook for 20 minutes. Remove the lid and place the asparagus on top. Cook for 5 minutes longer, until the asparagus is bright green and tender. Transfer the rice mixture to a large bowl along with the peas (they will quickly defrost in the mixture). Toss lightly using a fork to help separate the grains.

2   In a small bowl, whisk the lemon zest, lemon juice, and olive oil. Add this mixture to the rice mixture along with olives, dill, mint, salt, and pepper to taste, and mix.

3   To assemble, add the rice salad to 4 bento boxes or containers, then top with mozzarella, eggs or avocado cubes, and lemon wedges. Seal everything up and refrigerate until you are ready to take it with you.

4   Refrigerate again once you get to work, or keep it tucked away with a cooler pack. To serve, season with a squeeze of lemon and sprinkle of salt, then enjoy.

Falafel with Quinoa Tabbouleh

AND TAHINI-YOGURT DRESSING

The cookbook *Jerusalem* by Yotam Ottolenghi and Sami Tamimi was a gift from my dad many Christmases ago, and it was my first, and still my favorite, cookbook on the food of the region. The book used brand-new to me ingredient combinations for dishes that, to this day, turn out better than I could ever imagine, even after making them many times. Lucky me: I now live near all of Ottolenghi's eponymous delis in London, England, but it's a rare treat to visit one (being a responsible adult means watching your savings, I guess). The cuisine is one of the most striking in appearance, with emerald, mustard, cream, saffron, and ruby hues, all of which I've applied here to make this lunchtime ode to Middle Eastern cooking a feast for both the eyes and palate.

SERVES 4   ⧖ 12 HOURS SOAKING TIME; 45 MINUTES COOKING TIME   ⏱ 3 DAYS

1   For the falafel, preheat the oven to 425°F. Line a large rimmed baking sheet with parchment paper; grease the parchment with 2 tablespoons of olive oil.

2   In a food processor, pulse the garlic, parsley or arugula, flour, baking powder, cumin, coriander seeds, and salt until minced. Pulse in the lemon zest and juice and the remaining 1 tablespoon of olive oil. Drain the chickpeas and add to the food processor; pulse until finely minced and the mixture is just combined. Rest the mixture for 10 minutes to allow the flour to absorb the moisture.

3   Scoop the falafel mixture in approximately 3-tablespoon-sized portions onto the prepared baking sheet and gently form them into ½-inch-high discs (rough shapes are more than okay!). Bake for 10 to 12 minutes, until dry to the touch with a hint of browning on the bottoms. Set aside. Once cool, freeze falafels in a ziplock bag for up to 3 months.

CONTINUED

FALAFEL (MAKES 12)

3 Tbsp olive oil, divided

1 clove garlic

½ cup coarsely chopped fresh parsley or arugula

2 Tbsp flour (chickpea, wheat, spelt, etc.) or oat bran

1 tsp baking powder

1 tsp ground cumin

1 tsp whole coriander seeds

½ tsp salt

2 tsp lemon zest

2 Tbsp lemon juice

1 cup dry chickpeas, soaked for 12 hours in water

QUINOA TABBOULEH AND CUCUMBERS

2 cups water

1 cup quinoa

2 cups finely chopped fresh parsley

1 cup pomegranate seeds

1 green onion (white and green parts), minced

2 tsp lemon juice, plus lemon wedges for serving

1 tsp dried mint

4 Persian cucumbers, unpeeled and julienned or cubed

Sesame seeds

TAHINI-YOGURT DRESSING

⅔ cup plain whole-milk yogurt

½ cup tahini

¼ cup lemon juice

¼ tsp salt or 1 tsp gluten-free tamari

4   For the tabbouleh, in a medium saucepan, bring the water
    and quinoa to a boil, reduce to a simmer, cover, and cook for
    15 minutes. Let stand, covered, for another 5 minutes. Remove
    the lid, fluff with a fork, and cool for another 5 minutes. Stir in
    the parsley, pomegranate seeds, green onion, lemon juice, and
    mint, and chill until you are ready to assemble.

5   For the dressing, whisk the yogurt, tahini, lemon juice, and salt or
    tamari in a medium bowl until combined. If you prefer a thinner
    dressing, add water, 1 tablespoon at a time, until the dressing is
    the desired consistency. Transfer to an airtight container and
    refrigerate until you are ready to use, for up to 1 week.

6   To assemble, add a serving of tabbouleh to a bento box or
    container. Wrap up a few falafels in plastic, foil, or parchment
    paper to avoid sogginess if your container doesn't have separate
    compartments and add them to the container. Add a big
    spoonful of dressing to a small jar or small container, and tuck
    it beside the tabbouleh and falafels, followed by the cucumber,
    lemon wedges, and a sprinkle of sesame seeds. Seal and
    refrigerate until you are ready to take it with you.

7   Once you arrive at work, keep it chilled in the refrigerator or
    with a cooler pack in your lunch bag. To serve, season with
    lemon and enjoy chilled, or reheat the falafels in a low oven or
    toaster oven until warmed through and crisp, season with lemon,
    and eat.

Walnut-Crusted Avocado, Feta, and Eggs

WITH PESTO RICE

There are two tricks I use take this lunch box from ordinary to extraordinary. The first, tossing rice in pesto keeps it moist and tender for a few days, while helping to hold each grain's individuality. The second, crusting avocado in walnut crumble (or any crumbled nut or seed) helps it retain its green color and prevents it from becoming an unappetizing shade of brown. This lunch box's clarity and vibrant appeal comes through in every bite, making it a favorite around here.

SERVES 4   ⧖ 2 HOURS 30 MINUTES   ⟳ 4 DAYS

1   For the pesto rice, in a medium saucepan, bring the water and rice to a boil, reduce to a simmer, cover, and cook for 25 minutes. Turn off the heat and steam, covered, for 5 minutes. Remove the lid, fluff with a fork, and cool to room temperature before covering and refrigerating for at least 2 hours, until cold. Transfer the chilled rice to a large bowl and mix in the pesto and carrot (if using).

2   For the walnut-crusted avocado, add the walnut crumble to a large plate. Halve and pit the avocados, and scoop out the halves from the peel using a large spoon; discard the skin. Rub the avocado flesh all over with lemon juice and gently press the halves into the crumble to coat the sliced and peeled surface as fully as possible, including the pit indent.

3   To assemble, add a bed of pesto rice to each of 4 containers and top the rice with a walnut-crusted avocado half, along with the feta and egg. Sprinkle with cayenne and salt to taste. Seal everything up and refrigerate it until you are ready to take it with you.

4   If taking this to work, keep it in the refrigerator or with a cooler pack in your lunch bag until you are ready to open your container up and enjoy.

CONTINUED

PESTO RICE

1¼ cups water

1 cup medium-grain white rice

2 Tbsp No-Recipe Green Pesto (see Lunch Note) or prepared pesto

1 carrot, finely grated (optional)

WALNUT-CRUSTED AVOCADO, FETA, AND EGGS

½ cup Walnut Crumble (page 113)

4 avocados

Lemon juice, as needed

¾ cup crumbled feta cheese

4 hard-boiled eggs, peeled and halved

Cayenne

Salt

★ RESTYLE: MAKE IT A BOWL

Toss some arugula with lemon juice and olive oil and add it to 4 bowls. Mix the feta and cayenne into the rice and add it on top of the arugula mixture, followed by the walnut-crusted avocado and egg.

★ NO-RECIPE GREEN PESTO

I make pesto with a variety of tender green herbs like parsley, basil, arugula, cilantro, and even kale, stuffing them all in a food processor until it's nearly overflowing, along with a big clove of garlic, and pulsing until everything is minced. If I have pine nuts or walnuts handy, I add a handful of those, too, at this point. When everything is finely chopped, I turn on the machine and drizzle in extra-virgin olive oil, or a 50/50 mixture of extra-virgin olive oil and brown butter, until the mixture loosens up, resembling the consistency of a creamy salad dressing. To finish, I add a small squeeze of lemon juice or splash of sherry vinegar, along with a generous pinch of salt, and blend briefly one last time. I store the pesto in an airtight container in the freezer in small containers for 2 to 3 months, defrosting at room temperature when I need a pop of freshness. If you don't want to freeze the pesto, store it in a glass jar in the refrigerator for up to 1 week.

Lemon Roasted Potatoes, Chicken, and Spinach

WITH TZATZIKI

The riot of textures, colors, and flavors in this dish offers a visual and physical boost at noon. It's saladesque but eats heartier, rooted by sweet potatoes permeated with lemon, juicy chicken, tender spinach, briny olives, and cooling tzatziki to sauce it all. Enjoy as is today, and take along whole-grain pitas to fill or lavash to wrap for something different tomorrow.

SERVES 4   ⧖ 35 MINUTES   ⊙ 1 WEEK FOR LEMON
ROASTED POTATOES AND CHICKEN; 5 DAYS FOR TZATZIKI

1   For the sweet potatoes and chicken, preheat the oven to 400°F. On a large rimmed baking sheet, toss the sweet potatoes and chicken with the olive oil, lemon juice, salt, and pepper to taste. Roast for 15 to 20 minutes, until the chicken is tender and the juices run clear. Remove the chicken from the oven, transfer it to a cutting board to rest, and cook the sweet potatoes for 10 to 15 minutes longer, until they are very tender and beginning to brown. Cool the sweet potatoes before assembling the container.

2   For the tzatziki, use a spoon to scrape the seeds from the cucumber; discard them or save to use in smoothies or juices. Grate the cucumber and squeeze out the excess juice. Add the grated cucumber to a large bowl along with the yogurt, dill, mint, garlic, lemon juice, salt, and pepper to taste, and mix well to combine. Refrigerate in an airtight container for up to 1 week.

3   To assemble, slice the chicken crosswise or shred it using two forks. Add the spinach to each of 4 bento boxes or containers, then tuck in the chicken, sweet potatoes, tzatziki (or pack it separately), olives, and lemon wedges; drizzle with extra oil and sprinkle with the remaining dill. Seal and refrigerate until you are ready to take it with you. Keep chilled in the work refrigerator or with a cooler pack in your lunch bag. To serve, season with lemon and enjoy.

CONTINUED

LEMON ROASTED POTATOES AND CHICKEN

4 sweet potatoes, peeled and cut into ½-inch cubes

Four 4 oz boneless chicken breasts (skinless or skin-on)

¼ cup extra-virgin olive oil, plus more for serving

¼ cup lemon juice, plus lemon wedges for serving

½ tsp salt

Ground black pepper

8 cups baby spinach or baby arugula

1 cup kalamata olives

2 Tbsp chopped fresh dill

TZATZIKI

1 English cucumber, unpeeled and halved lengthwise

2 cups strained plain whole-milk yogurt or plain Greek yogurt (see Lunch Note)

¼ cup finely chopped fresh dill, plus more for serving

¼ cup finely chopped fresh mint

½ clove garlic, minced

1 Tbsp lemon juice

¼ tsp salt

Ground black pepper

* **MAKE STRAINED YOGURT AND TURN IT INTO LABNEH**

For Strained Yogurt

Line a large fine-mesh sieve with cheesecloth (approximately four 15-inch square layers), suspend it over a large bowl, and add 4 cups of plain yogurt (at least 2%, preferably whole milk). Refrigerate for at least 3 hours or up to 1 day. Transfer strained yogurt to a large container or clean yogurt container. Refrigerate as long as expiry date allows. You can refrigerate the whey (the liquid strained out of the yogurt) in a glass jar to use for marinades, dips, or dressings.

For Labneh

Follow the directions above, stirring ½ teaspoon of salt into the yogurt before straining.

* **RESTYLE: VEGETARIAN REVAMP**

Replace the chicken with cooked chickpeas, butter beans, or hard-boiled eggs. If you do use this substitute, don't roast your alternative protein of choice with the sweet potatoes as you do the chicken; just add it on top of the spinach as is.

Eggplant, Brown Rice, and Tahini Burgers

WITH A SALAD

If you love to meal prep for the week ahead, a step that's essential for a packed lunch, veggie burgers are one of the best ways to add a built-in-flavor-rich substance to your main course in a flash. Pop one on top of lettuce, pair it with crudités, use it to adorn a wild tangle of zucchini noodles or spaghetti squash—the options are boundless. In the summertime, I like to mix a robust salad, including some garden tomatoes, cucumbers, and herbs, to couple with a patty. But in all honesty, leaf lettuce, something that's easy to come by and doesn't take up a huge amount of real estate in the refrigerator, is more than enough, especially when generously splashed with a homemade dressing.

SERVES 4 (MAKES 8 BURGERS)   ⧗ 3 HOURS   ⊕ 3 DAYS

1   For the burgers, preheat the oven to 425°F. On a large rimmed baking sheet or glass or ceramic baking dish, place the eggplant and pierce it several times with a fork. Roast for 35 to 50 minutes, until the eggplant has darkened and collapsed. When it is cool enough to handle, scrape out the flesh into a fine-mesh sieve (a little skin is okay), suspend it over a bowl, and drain for 10 minutes. Discard the eggplant juices.

2   In a large bowl, add the drained eggplant and rice. Using clean hands, squish together the eggplant and rice until the mixture is evenly blended. Switch to a spatula or wooden spoon and mix in the tahini, almond flour, and garlic, followed by the pine nuts, raisins, olives, oregano, vinegar or lemon juice, salt, and nutmeg, and season the mixture with pepper. Cover and refrigerate the mixture for at least 2 hours and up to 1 day to firm up.

CONTINUED

1½ lb (1 regular) eggplant

1½ cups cold, cooked short-grain brown rice (page 241)

⅓ cup tahini

1 cup almond flour

2 cloves garlic, grated or minced

2 Tbsp pine nuts

2 Tbsp raisins, coarsely chopped

2 Tbsp (about 6) pitted, finely chopped kalamata olives

1 Tbsp finely chopped fresh oregano

2 tsp red wine vinegar or 1 Tbsp lemon juice

½ tsp salt

¼ tsp ground nutmeg

Ground black pepper

Red leaf lettuce, torn, for serving

Favorite green salad mix-ins, such as shredded savoy cabbage, sprouts, cucumber, shelled green peas, etc.

Plain Greek yogurt, for serving (optional)

Balsamic Vinaigrette (page 236) or Green Goddess Dressing (page 237), for serving, as needed

3   Arrange the oven racks to accommodate two trays. Preheat the
    oven to 450°F. Line 2 large baking sheets with parchment paper
    and scoop out the burger mixture (it will be tacky), evenly
    spacing it on baking sheets to make 8 patties. Using slightly wet
    hands, press the patties down until they are 1 inch thick. Bake
    for 10 minutes, then remove the baking sheets from the oven
    and gently flip each burger; rotate the trays when placing them
    back in the oven. Bake for 5 to 10 minutes longer, until both sides
    are golden brown and the patties are firm. Cool them before
    packing or storing them in the refrigerator or freezer (for up to
    2 months).

4   To assemble, add lettuce and salad mix-ins to 4 containers
    and top each with 2 burger patties and a dollop of yogurt (if
    using). Transfer the vinaigrette or dressing to a small airtight
    container or glass jar, seal, and tuck it into your salad container
    (if it doesn't fit, pack it on the side). Seal everything up and
    refrigerate until you are ready to take it with you. Keep cold in
    the work refrigerator or with a cooler pack in your lunch bag.
    Drizzle the salad with vinaigrette or dressing before enjoying.

Seasonal DIY Lunch Boxes

The physical layouts of lunch boxes are as diverse as what goes inside: locking glass containers, recycled takeout containers, tiffin boxes, recycled jam jars—they all work. If it seals tightly and is large enough for your meal, anything goes. Separate compartments in your box of choice are completely optional, but they do give your meal a hint of nostalgia while keeping wet and dry foods from mixing together.

Find your personal lunch box essentials in the Modern Meal Prep Staples chapter (page 235), and get building. Or choose a goal or mood listed below, and include the following components in amounts that feel right to you.

Balanced
combination of vegetables/fruit + whole grains + protein (omnivorous or plant-based) + healthy fats + and dressing/condiments

WINTER roasted butternut squash + steamed broccoli + brown rice + roasted salmon + balsamic vinaigrette

SPRING grilled asparagus + raw snap peas + quinoa + hard-boiled eggs + creamy caesar dressing

SUMMER mixed greens + cubed cucumber + baby tomatoes + toasted almonds + farro + grilled chicken + tahini-yogurt dressing

FALL kale salad + sliced apple + goat cheese + cooked barley + turkey meatballs + olive oil + lemon juice

Plant-Based
combination of vegetables/fruit + whole grains + protein (e.g., beans, tofu, hummus, lentils, nut butter) + healthy fats + crunch + dressing/condiments

WINTER roasted cauliflower + baby spinach + pickled red onion + sliced dates + flatbread + hummus + pine nuts + olive oil + lemon juice

SPRING carrot ribbons + asparagus ribbons + strawberries + soba noodles + marinated tofu + quinoa + roasted cashews + miso dressing

SUMMER crunchy chopped salad (yellow pepper, cucumber, raw beet, tomatoes, etc.) + edamame + avocado + brown rice + sesame seeds + crumbled nori + orange sesame dressing

FALL baked vegetables (squash, peppers, onions, turnips, parsnips, etc.) + toasted pita + falafel + tahini sauce + lemon juice

High-Protein

combination of vegetables + protein (omnivorous or plant-based) + healthy fats + low-sugar dressing/condiments

WINTER whole roasted sweet potato + steamed kale + poached chicken + coconut chips + coconut oil + tamari + lime juice

SPRING zucchini noodles + pesto + fresh mint + roasted salmon + white beans + olive oil + red wine vinegar

SUMMER shredded romaine + fresh tomato pico de gallo + chimichurri + black beans + grilled polenta + Greek yogurt

FALL roasted parsnips + kale salad + raisins + toasted walnuts + steak + spiced yogurt.

Low-Carb

combination of non-starchy vegetables + lean protein (e.g., salmon, hard-boiled eggs, chicken breast, steak, tofu) + healthy fats + condiments + low-sugar dressing/condiments

WINTER cauliflower "rice" + cilantro + avocado + baked portobello mushrooms + rice vinegar + olive oil

SPRING roasted fennel and leeks + blood orange + frittata + olive oil + lemon juice

SUMMER grilled zucchini + cherry tomatoes + red peppers + basil + arugula + burrata + dukkah

FALL slow-roasted tomatoes + kale chips + oil-packed tuna + black olives + toasted pine nuts + red wine vinegar

Low-Fat

combination of vegetables/fruit + whole grains + lean protein (e.g., chicken breast, canned tuna, Greek yogurt) + lower fat condiment/dressing

WINTER whole-grain pasta + roasted celery root + shredded radicchio + pomegranate seeds + Greek yogurt + pan-fried chickpeas + lemon juice

SPRING stir-fried spring vegetables + brown rice + ground turkey + toasted sesame oil + tamari

SUMMER miso-glazed eggplant + mixed greens + basmati rice + blueberries + grilled chicken + rice vinegar

FALL roasted delicata squash + green beans + couscous + baked chicken breast + feta + balsamic vinegar

Pantry Dal

WITH RAITA, BROWN RICE, AND MANGO

After a long day of apartment hunting in London, England, Geoff and I came back to our short-term rental craving a meal that would lift our spirits and comfort our senses. I made dal using dried lentils found in the pantry, spices found in the back of the cabinet, and a fresh lemon we had picked up at the shop around the corner. The meal was ready in under an hour, and it doubled as a packed lunch the following day as we set out to explore our new city again—this time, for fun.

SERVES 4   ⧖ 45 MINUTES   ⏱ 1 WEEK FOR DAL; 5 DAYS FOR RAITA

1   For the dal, in a large pot, heat the ghee, butter, or coconut oil over medium-high heat. Add the curry powder, mustard seeds, turmeric, ginger, chili flakes, and salt, and season with pepper. Fry for 30 seconds, until fragrant and the seeds are popping. Reduce the heat to medium-low and add the onion, garlic, and tamarind. Sauté until the onion is tender, 8 to 10 minutes. Stir in the lentils and then the water and bring to a boil, reduce the heat to low, cover, and cook for 25 to 30 minutes, stirring a few times, until the lentils are tender. Mix in 1 teaspoon of lemon juice if you are using tamarind and up to 3 teaspoons if using dates. Using an immersion blender, pulse a few times to puree about a third of the mixture (optional). Cool and store in an airtight container in the refrigerator for up to 1 week, or enjoy warm out of the pot right away.

2   For the raita, in a medium bowl, mix the cucumber, yogurt, dried mint, and salt. Refrigerate in an airtight container until you are ready to use.

CONTINUED

DAL

2 Tbsp ghee or butter or coconut oil

1 Tbsp mild curry powder

1 tsp black mustard seeds

1 tsp ground turmeric

½ tsp ground dried ginger

¼ tsp red chili flakes

¾ tsp salt

Ground black pepper

1 onion, finely diced

2 cloves garlic, finely diced

1 Tbsp tamarind or pitted dates, minced

1½ cups dried red lentils, rinsed and picked

5 cups water

1–3 tsp lemon juice, plus more for serving

RAITA, RICE, AND MANGO

½ English cucumber, unpeeled, grated, and liquid pressed (for 1 cup grated cucumber)

1 cup plain whole-milk yogurt

½ tsp dried mint

Pinch of salt

2 cups cooked long-grain brown (page 241) or white rice

2 small mangoes, cored, skin intact, cheeks scored into crosshatches

3   To assemble, for each serving, add a portion of dal, rice, raita, and mango to separate tiffin boxes or compartments in a bento box, or add a bed of rice to a container and top with dal, then pack the raita, mango, and additional lemon juice separately. Seal everything up and refrigerate until you are ready to take it with you. If taking this to work, keep in the refrigerator or with a cooler pack in your lunch bag until you are ready to reheat and eat.

4   To serve, if using stainless steel tiffin boxes, heat the dal and rice in a microwave-safe serving dish before serving, or heat directly in your microwave-safe container. Eat hot, with raita, mango (spoon it out of the skin), and additional lemon.

★ GRATE ADD-INS
Pardon the pun, but great dal add-ins are grated vegetables. Add grated sweet potato, carrot, or zucchini when sautéing the onion.

Soba Noodle Kit

WITH BOK CHOY AND TERIYAKI TOFU

The salad bar tofu at a very popular grocery chain was my first exposure to truly delicious sticky tofu. In this homemade version, teriyaki sauce creates a deep-red veneer on the outside of thin slabs of tofu when baked, doing double duty as the soba noodle dressing. If I'm eating this lunch at home, I add everything to a bowl, where I attempt (in private) to tackle it with chopsticks—messy but good. This is a cold noodle dish, so there's no need to reheat it, unless you'd like to.

SERVES 4   30 MINUTES   4 DAYS

1   For the teriyaki tofu, preheat the oven to 400°F. Line a large rimmed baking sheet with parchment paper; line the tofu up on the parchment. In a large bowl, whisk the hoisin, vinegar, miso, water, sesame oil, and garlic until combined. Spoon two-thirds of the sauce onto the tofu, turning to coat both sides; if a little pools on the parchment, that'll get nice and sticky in the oven, for glazing after baking. Bake for 10 minutes, flip, and bake for 10 minutes longer, until it is sticky and appears shellacked. Spoon any caramelized bits from the parchment while it is still warm.

2   For the soba noodles, bring a large pot of water to a boil and cook the noodles according to the package directions, until tender. Drain, rinse with cold water, and drain again. Add the noodles to the large bowl along with remaining one-third of the teriyaki sauce, tossing gently to combine.

3   For the bok choy, in a medium saucepan with a splash of water, steam the bok choy until tender and bright green, about 2 to 3 minutes. Transfer to a plate and sprinkle with sesame seeds.

4   To assemble, add the tofu, noodles, bok choy, and edamame to each of 4 containers or bento boxes. Seal everything up and refrigerate until you are ready to take it with you.

CONTINUED

TERIYAKI TOFU

1 package (12 oz) extra-firm tofu, pressed (page 84), cut into 12 thin triangles or rectangles

¼ cup gluten-free hoisin sauce

2 Tbsp rice vinegar

1 Tbsp white miso paste

1 Tbsp water

2 tsp toasted sesame oil

1 clove garlic, minced

SOBA NOODLES, BOK CHOY, AND EDAMAME

2 bundles (6½ oz) soba noodles (buckwheat noodles)

6 baby bok choy, halved

1 cup shelled, frozen edamame, defrosted

2 tsp sesame seeds (any color)

5   If you are taking this dish to work, keep it in the refrigerator or with a cooler pack in your lunch bag until you are ready to enjoy it. To serve it, grab a bite from each compartment, getting a different taste and texture every time. Or, toss all the components in a bowl and eat.

★ **HOW TO PRESS TOFU**

There's a lot of water in tofu, even the extra-firm varieties. When you press out some of that water, the tofu takes on a meatier texture that's ready to absorb any marinade or sauce you add to it, infusing it with flavor.

To press tofu (extra-firm varieties only: medium-firm, medium, soft, and silken varieties are too delicate), drain any water from the package, then wrap the tofu in a paper towel or clean kitchen towel and place it on a large serving plate. Place a small cutting board on top of the tofu, then weigh it down with a large can of tomatoes or anything else that will put pressure on it. Press the tofu for 30 minutes to 3 hours, then remove the weight and cutting board, unwrap the tofu, and discard the water on the plate. Your tofu is now ready to be marinated, sauced, baked, grilled, or fried—you name it! There are also commercial tofu presses available, but I don't own or use one.

Chicken, Eggplant, and Basil Wraps

WITH CASHEWS

A DIY lunch, especially one with edible dinnerware in the form of vegetable wraps, is soul-satisfying comfort food for me. Filling but not at all heavy—just on flavor—it works both inside and outside of the box for away and at home. A choice meal to share with your Modern Lunch Club (page 205).

This lunch box easily transforms to be vegetarian. See the Lunch Note for the perfect plant-based protein replacement.

SERVES 4 ⧗ 20 MINUTES ⏱ 5 DAYS

1 Tbsp coconut oil

1 lb ground chicken or 2 boneless, skinless chicken breasts pulsed in a food processor until minced

2 Chinese eggplants, sliced into thin rounds

Heaping ½ cup unsalted raw or roasted cashews

3 Tbsp rice vinegar

3 Tbsp gluten-free tamari or soy sauce

2 green onions (white and green parts), minced

2 cups coarsely torn basil leaves (use Thai basil if available)

1 head lettuce such as iceberg or Bibb, or cabbage, leaves separated

1   For the filling, in a large high-sided or nonstick skillet, heat the oil over medium heat. Add the chicken, eggplant, and cashews, and sauté until the chicken is cooked through and the eggplant is tender and browned, about 10 to 12 minutes. Stir in the vinegar and tamari or soy sauce, and cook for 1 minute longer, until the liquid is absorbed. Remove the skillet from the heat and stir in the green onion and basil. Transfer the filling to a large container or bowl, cool, seal or cover, and refrigerate until you are ready to assemble the wraps.

2   To assemble, divide the filling between 4 bento boxes or containers. Roll the lettuce leaves and tuck them in bento boxes or containers or securely wrap and pack on the side. Seal everything up and refrigerate until you are ready to take it with you.

3   When you arrive at work, keep your meal cold in the refrigerator or with a cooler pack in your lunch bag. To serve, keep the filling cold or reheat, if desired, then top the lettuce leaves with filling, tuck in the sides (like a taco), and enjoy.

★ MAKE IT VEGETARIAN

Replace the chicken with 1 package (12 ounces) extra-firm tofu, finely crumbled after pressing out the liquid (see How to Press Tofu, page 84). As it's already cooked, the tofu will only take about 5 minutes in the pan to dry out and become a touch crispy.

Black Bean Salsa Salad

WITH HOMEMADE CREPE TORTILLAS

Don't be scared off by the seemingly challenging task of making your own tortilla shells. If you can make pancakes, you can make these. Of course, there are many fine store-bought options that can stand in here (I keep a stash of La Tortilla Factory yellow and white corn tortillas—which I believe have the best texture, flavor, and durability—in my cupboard, for fast brunches, lunches, and dinners), but I do recommend keeping this crepe recipe on hand, if not for this meal, for any savory or sweet dish where you would use a thin pancake. Though not quite as sturdy as a flour or corn and wheat–blend tortilla, these tortillas offer a homemade option for those with celiac disease, like my sister, or a gluten intolerance. And if this is all just too fussy for you, the salsa salad is perfection on its own.

SERVES 4   ⧖ 25 MINUTES   ⟳ 4 DAYS

HOMEMADE CREPE TORTILLAS

(or use 8 small soft corn tortillas)

1 cup chickpea flour

2 Tbsp gluten-free all-purpose flour

¼ tsp salt

1 cup water

¼ cup plain whole-milk yogurt

BLACK BEAN SALSA SALAD

One 19 oz can black beans, drained and rinsed

1 avocado, pitted, peeled, and diced

1 cup quartered cherry tomatoes

⅔ cup fresh or frozen corn kernels

½ bell pepper, any color, seeded and diced

½ cup chopped fresh cilantro

1 green onion (white and green parts), diced

2 Tbsp extra-virgin olive oil

1 Tbsp lime juice

1 jalapeño, seeded and minced (optional)

½ tsp salt

1   For the tortillas, in a medium bowl, whisk the flours and salt to combine. Whisk in the water and yogurt and set aside for 10 minutes to allow the flours to absorb the water and the mixture to thicken slightly.

2   To cook, use a paper towel to wipe a thin layer of oil in a small nonstick pan. Spoon a scant ¼ cup of batter into the pan, swirling it into a thin circle as you would cook a crepe. Cook for 1 minute, until bubbles appear on top and a few light brown spots appear on the underside; flip and cook the other side for 30 seconds longer, until a few light brown spots appear on the underside and the edges appear dry. Transfer to a plate. Repeat with remaining batter. Cool completely and store in an airtight container at room temperature until you are ready to pack.

3   For the salad, add the beans, avocado, cherry tomatoes, corn, bell pepper, cilantro, green onion, olive oil, lime juice, jalapeño to taste, and salt to a large bowl and mix to combine.

4   To assemble, divide the salad between 4 containers or bento boxes. Seal and refrigerate until you are ready to take it with you. Pack the tortillas separately and keep them at room temperature to keep them from drying and cracking.

5   If you are taking this dish to work, keep the salad in the refrigerator or stored with a cooler pack in your lunch bag until you are ready to eat it. To serve, fill the tortillas with salad, tear tortillas over the salad, or use pieces of tortilla to scoop up the salad, and enjoy.

PART II

LUNCH AT HOME

(though nearly all packable)

WORKING FROM HOME, as I do, requires weekday lunches at home. You'll need the same if you live close enough to your workplace to walk home for lunch. Or if you freelance. Or are doing shift work. Or took a day off. Or are on parental leave. Or are retired. Or attend school. Weekday lunch at home feels playful, especially when it's packable food presented outside a container or jar. But rest assured, there's no short-order cooking; almost all of these recipes can be taken to go, so every member of the house has something to eat (or, if it's just you, tomorrow you could be at work/away/driving/on a plane and need a packed lunch—I don't know your life!).

Lunch at home also happens on the weekend. Weekend lunches at home, with the sunlight trickling into our kitchen, are something I look forward to all week long, and are made even better if the weather is warm enough to eat outside. The weekend is also a time for families to get together without having to rush off to after-school activities, do homework or, unlike dinner, worry about

bedtime immediately after the dishes. When I was growing up, my parents would arrange deli meats, cheeses, lettuce, tomatoes, mayonnaise, and mustard on a lazy Susan, along with halved Kaiser buns bought that morning, allowing us to build our own sandwiches. It taught us all to slow down, if only for 20 minutes, and try to make a Saturday or Sunday family meal materialize, at least one weekend afternoon a month.

In this section, you'll find freshened up plates, balanced salads that will fill you up for the afternoon, and beautiful bowls. And, as I mentioned above, most of the following recipes here are designed to be packable, all without compromising taste, texture, or appearance. The helpful "packable" icon at the top of the page will indicate the recipe's to-go status where appropriate, and my notes in the recipe's method will instruct you on how to pack it up for the best flavor, texture, and durability. These meals are suitable for any and every day of the week, wherever you call home.

CHAPTER 4

Plates and Bowls

I WAS INTRODUCED TO the concept of plates a few years ago (which sounds so silly when I actually write it down) in Montreal, and again in Venice Beach. Plates are uncluttered, uncomplicated food that can be presented with each component arranged on its own dish; spread across a table to be served build-your-own, family-style; or presented with a variety of components arranged on a single plate, with no DIY-ing involved (unless you're cooking).

I turn to plates on a workday as something I can graze over while typing away, but they function just as well on a summer weekend when I'm flipping through a magazine or good book, or scrolling through my Instagram feed (@allisondaycooks) outside.

Plates are okay with not being the center of attention, which is why I love them so much for lunch, a meal that generally feels more casual than dinner anyway. They can be (and often are in my house) combined with another recipe or a small no-recipe recipe, like a quick side salad, a cooked grain or vegetable, some toasted sourdough drenched in olive oil, or an unfussy protein option. Mixing, matching, and adding to your plate-focused meal is encouraged! Have enough food out to satisfy your appetite and don't be afraid to reload.

And bowl food is something I have written extensively about—like in my first cookbook, *Whole Bowls*. Years later, I still find them the perfect way to eat midday, so I've included a couple of new, complete meal bowl recipes that are packable and don't require reheating.

This chapter's recipes are nearly all portable, making them a weekday-friendly option, as well as a more elegant yet laid-back lunch to share on a weekend.

California Lunch Bowl

While writing this book, I finally ventured to California, and it became a new "happy place" for me. Gjusta, a bakery and restaurant in Venice Beach, California, has a grain bowl that played with temperature, texture, and flavor in a way I'd never experienced before and needed to recreate immediately upon my return home. The soft egg in this bowl, like the one I enjoyed at Gjusta, marries with the lightest, clearest dressing for an expression of modern healthy eating that I believe anyone can get behind.

SERVES 2 ⋄ 10 MINUTES ⋄ 1 DAY

1 For the poached eggs, fill a small skillet two-thirds full of water. Add the white vinegar, bring the water to a boil, and crack in the eggs. Immediately remove from the heat and cover for 7 minutes. If you are taking this to go, use a hard-boiled egg (page 238) instead of a poached egg.

2 To assemble, to serving bowls, add the rice, romaine, fennel, and avocado. Season with the olive oil, balsamic vinegar, salt and pepper to taste, and chili. Top with the dukkah and cilantro. Remove the egg from the water with a slotted spoon, draining as much water as possible; place on top of the rice. Toss, allowing the yolk to become part of the dressing, and enjoy. If you are packing this to go, assemble your bowl in a container replacing the poached egg with a peeled hard-boiled egg. Seal and refrigerate until you are ready to take it with you, and keep it refrigerated at work or chilled with a cooler pack until you are ready to eat.

★ **KEEP SLICED AVOCADO FRESH**
To keep avocado from browning, concentrate the olive oil and balsamic vinegar on the avocado flesh, and then sprinkle dukkah over top to cover. This assembly trick keeps oxidation to a minimum.

1 Tbsp distilled white vinegar

2 large eggs

2 cups cooked brown rice (page 241) or quinoa (page 242), preferably warm

2 cups shredded romaine lettuce

¼ bulb fennel, shaved

1 avocado, halved, peeled, and sliced

2 Tbsp extra-virgin olive oil

1 Tbsp balsamic vinegar

Salt

Ground black pepper

1 tsp minced fresh red Thai chili

2 Tbsp dukkah (page 168)

¼ cup chopped fresh cilantro

Baked Squash

WITH BROWN BUTTER, FETA, AND CHILI

This recipe is versatile and vibrant. It can be scaled up for a crowd or for leftovers, which, beyond lunch, taste great smashed onto toast or mixed into savory steel-cut oats for breakfast the next day. To complete the meal, I like to serve the baked squash with a rustic sourdough bread or a cooked whole grain like barley or quinoa for sopping up the juices, along with a simple side salad of tender baby lettuces lightly coated with lemon juice, olive oil, and flaky salt. If you're searching for crunch to contrast with the tender squash, a sprinkle of chopped nuts or toasted coconut chips before serving is just the ticket.

SERVES 4 AS A SIDE ⧖ 40 MINUTES ⏱ 3 DAYS

1 Preheat the oven to 375°F. In a medium saucepan, heat the butter over medium heat until it is golden brown and nutty in aroma, about 5 to 8 minutes. Immediately transfer it to a small bowl, including the brown bits, which have a lot of great flavor. In a 9- × 13-inch ceramic or glass baking dish, coat the squash, onion, garlic, chili, and ginger with the brown butter. Place the squash cup side-up and add a slab of feta to each piece.

2 Bake for 35 to 45 minutes, until the squash is tender and the feta is beginning to brown. Fire it under the broiler for a minute, watching carefully, for a deeper golden-brown color on the feta, if desired.

3 If you are eating this immediately, drizzle the squash with honey, sprinkle it with cilantro, and garnish with additional chili. Serve warm.

4 If you are taking this to go, pack a serving in a container and refrigerate it until you are ready to take it with you. Keep it in the work refrigerator or stored with a cooler pack in your lunch bag until you are ready to reheat, if desired, and eat it.

¼ cup unsalted butter

One 2–3 lb red kuri or buttercup or kabocha squash, seeded, peeled, and sliced into 8 large pieces

1 onion, sliced

2 cloves garlic, peeled and sliced

1 red Thai chili, seeded and minced, plus more for garnish

1 Tbsp minced fresh ginger

6 oz feta, thickly sliced into 8 slabs

1 Tbsp honey

¼ cup torn fresh cilantro

★ BUMP UP THE PROTEIN

Add a bed of 2 cups of cooked white beans or chickpeas and splash of water (or white wine) to the bottom of your baking dish before topping with squash and baking. Or nestle 4 raw turkey sausages in between the squash before baking; they will cook in the same amount of time as everything else.

Modern Ploughman's Lunch

A composed plate from the midday meal eaten by English farm workers, the ploughman's lunch traditionally consists of a hunk of bread, some cheese, and an apple. Pickles, eggs, and meat pies are often added, but at its core, the ploughman's lunch remains simple, satisfying, and portable. In this updated version, I've made a rich vegetarian pâté—which really does taste like traditional liver pâté! you must try it!—in lieu of the traditional meat pie. The from-scratch pâté is not only easier to prepare than a from-scratch meat pie but also far healthier. This plate's ingredients sparkle in their clarity, so choose the best of each you can access.

SERVES 4   ⧗ 6 HOURS 20 MINUTES   ⊕ 2 WEEKS FOR CHICKPEA WALNUT PÂTÉ

1   For the pâté, heat the oil in a large skillet over medium heat. Add the onion, garlic, rosemary, sage, cloves, and salt, and season with pepper. Reduce the heat to medium-low and sauté for 8 to 10 minutes, until the onions are cooked and beginning to brown. Add the vermouth or apple juice and cook until it has evaporated, about 30 seconds. Remove from the heat and stir in the vinegar.

2   Add the onion mixture to a food processor with the chickpeas, walnuts, and mustard. Pulse to incorporate. Add the butter and blend, scraping down the sides once or twice, until the mixture is mostly smooth (a few unblended walnut pieces will probably remain, which I like!). Pulse in the parsley.

3   Line a loaf pan (about 6 × 4 inches) or small mixing bowl with plastic wrap, leaving plenty of overhang. Smooth in the pâté, making sure to remove air pockets. Bring up the sides and seal, pressing gently. Refrigerate for at least 6 hours, preferably 12 hours.

4   To cut, remove the pâté from the pan, unwrap, and slice it (cleaning the knife between each slice) into thick slabs. Only slice what you need. Rewrap and refrigerate for up to 2 weeks.

CONTINUED

CHICKPEA WALNUT PÂTÉ

1 Tbsp extra-virgin olive oil

1 cup diced onion

1 clove garlic, minced

½ tsp chopped fresh or dried rosemary

½ tsp chopped fresh or dried sage

⅛ tsp ground cloves

½ tsp salt

Ground black pepper

2 Tbsp sweet vermouth or apple juice

2 tsp sherry vinegar or apple cider vinegar

One 19 oz can or 2 cups cooked chickpeas, drained and rinsed

1 cup walnut halves

2 tsp Dijon mustard

¼ cup unsalted butter, room temperature

1 Tbsp finely chopped fresh parsley

PLATE

1 apple

Dijon mustard

4 hard-boiled eggs, peeled and halved

6 oz aged white cheese of choice, sliced

8 peeled baby carrots

1 package (150 g) whole-grain nut and fruit crackers, gluten-free if necessary

1 small sheet or 1 small pot honeycomb or honey

1 cup sprouts or 1 head little gem lettuce leaves

5   To assemble, if eating at home, slice the apple. To 4 plates, add a smear of mustard, slice of pâté (you will likely have leftovers), 2 egg halves, cheese, apple, carrots, crackers, a piece of honeycomb or pool of honey, side of sprouts or lettuce, and then serve. If you are taking this to go, keep the apple whole and pack it on the side, and add a portion of the remaining components to an airtight bento-style divided container, keeping the dry and wet ingredients separate, then seal and refrigerate it until you are ready to take it with you. Keep it in the work refrigerator or tucked away with a cooler pack in your lunch bag until you're ready for lunch, then slice the apple and enjoy.

★ **PLOUGHMAN'S PLATTER**

Build a weekend entertaining ploughman's platter instead of individual plates. Serve all components family-style and see guests create their own interpretation of this traditional English midday meal. Bump up the portions as needed.

Baked Sweet Potatoes

WITH 4 DIFFERENT TOPPINGS

I began making topped sweet potatoes in university. They made for an easy and healthy lunch, and I could cap them with coconut oil, steamed spinach, and a poached egg before heading off to class for the afternoon. That was a great combo, but I've provided some more zhuzhed up suggestions below. Beyond these ideas, look to sandwiches or salads for inspiration, like chicken club, black bean taco, or fattoush.

Each topping recipe is enough for 1 baked sweet potato. Prepare the full amount of plain sweet potatoes for the week, as they keep well.

EACH TOPPING SERVES 1 ⧗ 45 MINUTES ⏱ 5 DAYS FOR SWEET POTATOES; 1 DAY FOR TOPPED SWEET POTATOES

1 Preheat the oven to 400°F.

2 Line a large rimmed baking sheet with parchment paper.

3 Scrub sweet potatoes, poke them all over with a paring knife, and place on the prepared baking sheet. Bake for 45 minutes to 1 hour 30 minutes (depending on their size), flipping it halfway through the cooking time, until tender when pierced with a knife, and the juices have begun to caramelize. Use as directed in recipe or cool and store in an airtight container in the refrigerator for up to 5 days.

Toppings

MEDITERRANEAN SARDINE On a plate or in a container, open the sweet potato lengthwise to create a jacket. Top it with 1 cup of steamed kale, ½ cup of halved cherry tomatoes, 2 cooked sardines (from a can), and 1 teaspoon of minced fresh chili. Season with salt, pepper, olive oil, and lemon juice. Enjoy immediately or refrigerate the container for up to 1 day to take for tomorrow's lunch.

CONTINUED

TAHINI YOGURT, SPINACH, AND POMEGRANATE On a plate or in a container, open the sweet potato lengthwise to create a jacket. In a small bowl, combine 1 tablespoon each of yogurt, tahini, and lemon juice, 1 teaspoon of water, and ½ teaspoon of tamari. Top the sweet potato with 1 cup of steamed spinach, ½ cup of cooked chickpeas, the tahini mixture, 1 tablespoon of pomegranate seeds, and 2 tablespoons of chopped cilantro. Season with olive oil and lemon juice. Enjoy immediately or refrigerate the container for up to 1 day to take for tomorrow's lunch.

CURRIED TURKEY In a large high-sided skillet, heat 1 teaspoon of butter or coconut oil over medium heat. Sauté ¼ onion, sliced, ½ clove of minced garlic, ¾ teaspoon of curry powder, ¼ teaspoon of ground turmeric, ⅛ teaspoon of salt, and ground black pepper to taste until the onion begins to brown, about 5 minutes. Add ¼ pound of ground turkey and sauté, breaking it up into small pieces, until it is cooked through and beginning to brown, 8 to 10 minutes. Stir in 1 tablespoon of chicken broth or water and 1 teaspoon of lemon juice; cook for another minute until the mixture is bubbling. On a plate or in a sealable container, open the sweet potato lengthwise to create a jacket. Top the potato with the turkey mixture, a dollop each of plain Greek yogurt and mango chutney, and a scattering of fresh cilantro or mint. Enjoy immediately or refrigerate the container for up to 1 day to take for tomorrow's lunch.

CHICKEN, CAULIFLOWER, DATE, AND SUMAC On a plate or sealable container, open the sweet potato lengthwise to create a jacket. Top with 4 ounces of cooked chicken (page 239), ½ cup of chopped leftover roasted cauliflower, 1 pitted chopped medjool date, 1 tablespoon of chopped fresh mint, 1 tablespoon of toasted pine nuts, and thinly sliced red onion to taste. Season with olive oil, lemon juice, and a generous sprinkle of sumac. Enjoy immediately or refrigerate the container for up to 1 day to take for tomorrow's lunch.

Pink and Green
New Potato Salad

WITH SMOKED TROUT

PINK AND GREEN NEW POTATO SALAD

1½ lb medium new potatoes

1 bunch radishes, quartered

¼ cup mayonnaise

Zest of 1 lemon

3 Tbsp lemon juice, plus more for serving

1 Tbsp Dijon mustard

2 green onions (white and green parts), minced

¼ cup finely chopped fresh dill, plus more for serving

¼ tsp salt

Ground black pepper

ENDIVE, SMOKED TROUT, AND EGGS

1 head endive, leaves separated

1 whole hot-smoked trout or 2 sides hot-smoked trout fillets, skin and bones removed, flaked into large pieces

4 hard-boiled eggs, peeled and halved

There's a very special spot in Montreal called Larry's that offers a selection of contemporary Nordic-meets-Jewish-meets-French small dishes, lunches, and brunches. Geoff and I went for the great coffee, but stayed for lunch when we saw the perfect plates coming out of the kitchen and landing on the tables around us. This recipe, inspired by Larry's, is a beautiful, fresh way to dine midday on a weekend, although it transitions seamlessly to a workday lunch thanks to its superior packability.

SERVES 4   ⏳ 40 MINUTES   ⏱ 4 DAYS FOR POTATO SALAD

1   For the potato salad, steam or boil the potatoes until tender. When they are cool enough to handle, cube the potatoes and add them to a large bowl along with the radishes.

2   In a medium bowl, whisk to combine the mayonnaise, lemon zest, lemon juice, mustard, green onion, dill, salt, and pepper to taste. Add to the potatoes and radishes and fold to combine. Cover and refrigerate until you are ready to serve.

3   To assemble, if you are eating immediately, arrange the potato salad, endive leaves, trout, and eggs on a plate. Garnish with additional lemon and dill, and serve. If taking it to go, for each lunch container, add a serving of potato salad, endive leaves, trout, and eggs, along with additional lemon and dill, then seal and refrigerate it until you are ready to take it with you. When you get to work, refrigerate it again in the refrigerator or keep it chilled with a cooler pack in your lunch bag. Enjoy chilled.

Sheet-Pan Persian Lemon Chicken

When I think of, and subsequently, crave, Persian cuisine, I pull out all the spice stops, found here in the form of heady cinnamon, almost-sour sumac, and luscious cardamom. And while the ingredient list may seem long, this meal can be assembled in 5 to 10 minutes. I skip plating each component and plunk the whole tray, hot from the oven, in the center of the table so that my guests can embrace lunchtime community in its richest form.

SERVES 4 ⧗ 50 MINUTES ⏱ 4 DAYS

1   Preheat the oven to 400°F. On a large rimmed baking sheet, place the chicken pieces or breasts, potatoes, sweet potatoes, garlic, and onion. Juice the lemon over everything and toss on the juiced whole lemon half, along with the olive oil, sumac, cumin, thyme, cinnamon, cardamom, and salt. Season with pepper. Toss everything thoroughly with clean hands. Spread the mixture into a single layer with the chicken skin facing up.

2   Roast for 45 minutes, or until the chicken is cooked through and crispy-skinned, registering 160°F to 165°F on an instant-read thermometer with the juices running clear, and the potatoes are tender. Discard the lemon half.

3   As soon as the tray is out of the oven, top the tray bake with the spinach, dollops of yogurt, pomegranate seeds, and a drizzle of pomegranate molasses (if using), and serve.

CONTINUED

One 4 lb fresh whole chicken, cut into 8 pieces, or 4 bone-in, skin-on chicken breasts, halved

3 Yukon Gold potatoes, quartered

1 sweet potato, cut into 1-inch pieces

3 cloves garlic, smashed, kept whole

1 onion, quartered

½ lemon

¼ cup extra-virgin olive oil

1 Tbsp sumac

½ tsp cumin seed or ground cumin

½ tsp dried thyme

¼ tsp ground cinnamon

¼ tsp ground cardamom

½ tsp salt

Ground black pepper

2 cups baby spinach

½ cup plain whole-milk yogurt

½ cup pomegranate seeds

Pomegranate molasses, for drizzling (optional)

4   If you are taking this to go, you have 2 options: to enjoy this meal warm or cold. To serve it warm, cool the tray bake slightly, add a serving to a container, and drizzle it with pomegranate molasses, to taste. Pack the spinach, yogurt, and pomegranate seeds on the side. Seal and refrigerate it until you are ready to take it with you, up to 4 days. Keep it in the refrigerator at work or with a cooler pack in your lunch bag until you are ready to reheat it, then top it with the spinach, dollops of yogurt, and pomegranate seeds, and serve.

5   To serve it cold, add a serving to a container and top it with the spinach, dollops of yogurt, pomegranate seeds, and a drizzle of pomegranate molasses, to taste. Seal and refrigerate it until you are ready to take it with you, up to 4 days. Keep it in the refrigerator at work or with a cooler pack in your lunch bag until you are ready to eat it.

Brussels Sprout, Grape, and Goat Cheese Pizza

The no-knead method for pizza dough, which was made famous by pizza prince Jim Lahey, is the fail-proof method I always use. Combined with the Martha Stewart cast-iron-pan pizza method and a hot oven, a better-for-you and better-than-takeout option for lunch can be yours, hot, warm, at room temperature, or even cold. See the Lunch Note for more topping ideas.

The dough needs a full 18 to 24 hours to rise (all hands-off time), so start 1 to 2 days in advance. Once the dough is ready, pizza on demand is on the table in under 30 minutes.

SERVES 4   ⏳ 24 HOURS 30 MINUTES   🕐 3 DAYS

1   For the dough, in a large bowl, combine the flour, salt, and yeast. Stir in the water and mix until fully combined (using your hands to finish mixing is easiest). Oil the dough and place it in a bowl. Cover the bowl with a clean, slightly damp cloth and let it sit at room temperature for 18 to 24 hours, ideally somewhere away from cool drafts, such as on the top of your refrigerator or in your pantry. Store in an airtight container in the refrigerator for up to 3 days; bring the dough to room temperature before handling it.

2   For the pizzas, preheat the oven to 450°F. Sprinkle a clean surface with a bit of flour. Punch down the dough in the bowl and transfer it to the floured surface. Divide the dough into 4 balls using a pair of clean scissors.

3   Sprinkle a large cast-iron skillet with cornmeal. Working with 1 dough ball at a time, on your floured surface with floured hands, slowly stretch the dough out as thin as possible without ripping it. The center should ideally be ⅛ to 1/16 inch thick (be patient here), but leave the outer crust a bit thicker. Finish stretching the dough in a cornmeal-coated skillet.

4   Evenly scatter a quarter of the Brussels sprouts and grapes over the dough and gently press them into the dough. Add ¼ cup of

CONTINUED

DOUGH

18 oz (3¾ cups) unbleached all-purpose flour, plus more for shaping

2 tsp salt

¼ tsp active dry yeast

1½ cups water

Extra-virgin olive oil, for greasing

PIZZA

4 Tbsp instant cornmeal

2 cups thinly sliced Brussels sprouts

2 cups seedless red or green grapes, halved

1 cup fresh goat cheese

Salt

Ground black pepper

Extra-virgin olive oil

the cheese in dollops and season with salt, pepper, and olive oil. Bake for 15 to 20 minutes, until the pizza begins to brown on the outside and crisp on the bottom.

5   To serve, loosen the crust with a bread knife and carefully slide the pizza onto a cutting board. Drizzle it with more olive oil, slice, and serve. Repeat with the remaining dough balls and toppings.

6   If taking the pizza to go, seal each cooled pizza in plastic wrap or foil and refrigerate until you are ready to take it with you. Refrigerate it again at work or keep it chilled with a cooler pack until you're ready to reheat the pizza in a toaster oven or microwave until hot (it will still taste great but will lose crispiness in the microwave), and enjoy. Or eat the pizza cold.

★ NAAN CRUST PIZZA

My sister-in-law Katie told me about using prepared naan as a pizza crust. I think this is a brilliant idea. Make a few at a time on a large rimmed baking sheet lined with parchment paper or foil, and bake them until the toppings are bubbling and brown and the naan is crispy on the bottom.

★ PIZZA TOPPINGS

Use a light hand on the toppings to avoid a soggy, floppy crust, but go heavy on the creativity. Here are some doable-at-home pizza combos that I'm a fan of:

· simple tomato sauce + basil + mozzarella
· spicy tomato sauce + cooked bacon + egg
· mushroom + lemon zest + manchego + rosemary
· apple + bacon + béchamel + sage
· squash + ricotta + nutmeg + honey
· labneh + lemon zest + roasted garlic + pomegranate molasses
· kale + goat cheese + black olives + pine nuts
· prosciutto + pear + parmesan + thyme
· fig jam + blue cheese + arugula (top with raw arugula after baking)
· roasted red peppers + hummus + walnuts
· cream cheese + smoked salmon + capers + lemon (all added raw after baking the crust)

Avocado with Turmeric Yogurt and Walnut Crumble

Sometimes it's good to rein things in and lighten up lunch. When I need a big boost of nutrition, I turn to avocados, featured here in their purest form. This recipe works best as a side plate at lunch but can be easily added to and amped up. For a bowl option, add meal prep staples such as shredded poached chicken, hard-boiled eggs, white beans, or cubed smoked tofu, along with a big scoop of brown or sticky rice. Or keep things simple with a juicy fillet of roasted salmon, which marries nicely with this recipe's mellow tastes and exciting textures.

SERVES 4 AS A SIDE ⊠ 20 MINUTES ⏱ 1 TO 6 MONTHS FOR WALNUT CRUMBLE; 1 WEEK FOR TURMERIC YOGURT

1   For the walnut crumble, place the walnut halves, thyme, ginger, coriander seeds, and salt in a food processor or the bowl of a large mortar and pestle, and pulse or crush until finely chopped. Add the mixture to a large skillet and toast over medium-low heat for 5 to 10 minutes, until fragrant. Set aside. Cool and store in an airtight container at room temperature for up to 1 month or refrigerate for up to 6 months.

2   For the turmeric yogurt, in a medium bowl, combine the yogurt, lemon juice, miso, maple syrup or honey, turmeric, tamari, and pepper. Store in an airtight container in the refrigerator until you are ready to assemble the dish, up to 1 week.

3   For the cucumber and avocado, use a vegetable peeler or mandolin to shave the cucumber into ribbons. Pit, halve, and scoop out the avocados, discarding the pits and skin.

4   To assemble, spoon half of the yogurt onto 4 plates, top with the cucumber and avocado, and sprinkle with walnut crumble. Serve with additional yogurt and olive oil for dressing at the table, and a sprinkle of edible flowers (if using).

WALNUT CRUMBLE

1 cup walnut halves

¼ tsp dried thyme

¼ tsp dried ground ginger

¼ tsp whole coriander seeds

¼ tsp salt

TURMERIC YOGURT, CUCUMBER, AND AVOCADO

1 cup plain Greek yogurt, preferably whole milk

2 Tbsp lemon juice

1½ Tbsp white miso paste

1 Tbsp maple syrup or honey

1 tsp ground dried turmeric

½ tsp gluten-free tamari

⅛ tsp ground black pepper

1 English cucumber, unpeeled

2–4 avocados

Extra-virgin olive oil, for serving

Edible flowers, for serving (optional)

Triple Beet and Smoked Mackerel Grain Bowl

A nod to my Danish heritage, first book, and blog name, this is very much what I would order if it were presented to me on a menu. I'm hoping it fits you like a glove, too.

SERVES 4   ⧖ 1 HOUR 15 MINUTES   ⟳ 1 DAY ASSEMBLED; 1 WEEK SEPARATED

ROASTED BEETS, BEET GREENS, AND BEET HORSERADISH YOGURT

1 large bunch beets (4–6 beets) with beet greens intact

Salt

1 cup plain whole-milk yogurt

1 Tbsp Beet Horseradish Relish (page 236) or 1 Tbsp prepared beet horseradish

BROWN RICE, MACKEREL, AND CUCUMBERS

2 cups cooked warm or cold brown rice (page 241) or your favorite cooked grain

Two 8 oz smoked mackerel or smoked trout fillets, flaked

½ English cucumber, unpeeled and thinly sliced into coins

Extra-virgin olive oil, for serving

2 Tbsp finely chopped fresh dill

Ground black pepper

Lemon wedges, for serving

1 For the beets and beet greens, preheat the oven to 400°F. Remove the beet greens from the beets and set aside. Wrap the beets in foil and roast them for 45 minutes to 1 hour, or until they are tender when pierced with a knife. Unwrap the foil and let the beets cool until you can comfortably handle them. Peel and quarter the beets and set aside.

2 Slice the reserved beet greens, including the pink stems, into thin shreds. Rinse the greens well to remove all grit, and leave some water clinging to the greens to help them steam. Cover and steam the beet greens and stems in a large skillet over high heat for 2 to 3 minutes, until wilted and tender. Remove from the heat, uncover, and mix in the quartered beets. Season everything with salt.

3 For the beet horseradish yogurt, to a medium bowl, add the yogurt and relish or horseradish and mix well.

4 To serve, add the brown rice, beet greens, quartered beets, mackerel, and cucumber to bowls. Spoon on some beet horseradish yogurt, drizzle with olive oil, sprinkle with dill and pepper to taste, and serve with lemon wedges.

5 If you are taking this to go, for one portion, add a serving each of brown rice, beet greens, quartered beets, mackerel, and cucumber to a container. Spoon on some beet horseradish yogurt, drizzle with olive oil, sprinkle with dill and pepper to taste, and tuck in a lemon wedge for seasoning. Seal and refrigerate until you are ready to take it with you. Keep it in the refrigerator or with a cooler pack in your lunch bag until you are ready to eat.

CHAPTER 5

Salads with Substance

LUNCH AND SALAD go hand in hand, but I take a far more modern approach to their assembly. Salad for lunch needs to be nutritionally balanced and wholly satisfying—it cannot leave you looking for a sandwich to fill the gap. These recipes, toss (pardon the pun) the concept of lettuce-plus-dressing aside, focusing on ingredients and preparation techniques that work for you. Many can be made completely ahead and all are packable.

I recommend choosing two recipes per week, one grain-based and one vegetable-based, and having two salads for lunch every day. This not only keeps boredom out of the equation, it's more salad bar–style to boot and each will serve you a day or two longer.

If you crave more protein in your salad, you'll find a trove of essential recipes on pages 238–43 for grilled, poached, roasted, marinated, and ready-to-go meat and vegetarian-friendly options; likewise for nourishing whole grains.

Mustard Seed
Roasted Vegetable, Barley, and Bean Salad

A substantial, complete meal salad that's as simple to plate as it is to pack: just scoop and dive in. Or assemble it into a layered jar meal (see Lunch Note). Perk up leftovers with an extra drizzle of balsamic or squeeze of lemon.

SERVES 4   ⏳ 45 MINUTES   🕐 4 DAYS

MUSTARD SEED ROASTED VEGETABLES

½ butternut squash, peeled and cut into ½-inch cubes

2 red bell peppers, seeded and cut into 1-inch pieces

1 onion, sliced lengthwise into small wedges

2 Tbsp olive oil

2 tsp black mustard seeds

¼ tsp salt

BARLEY, BEANS, AND DRESSING

½ cup uncooked pearl barley

One 19 oz can cannellini beans, drained and rinsed

2 cups finely shredded kale or Swiss chard

2 Tbsp balsamic vinegar

1 Tbsp extra-virgin olive oil

1 Tbsp gluten-free tamari or soy sauce

1   For the roasted vegetables, preheat the oven to 400°F. Add the squash, peppers, onion, olive oil, mustard seeds, and salt to a large rimmed baking sheet. Roast for 40 to 45 minutes, until the vegetables are tender and beginning to brown. Transfer to a large bowl.

2   For the barley, beans, and dressing, in a medium saucepan, cover the barley with 3 inches of water, bring to a boil, reduce the heat to medium-low, and cook uncovered for 20 to 25 minutes, until tender. Drain, rinse with cold water, and drain again.

3   To a large bowl, add the barley, roasted vegetables, beans, kale or chard, vinegar, olive oil, and tamari or soy sauce. Toss well to combine. Taste and season with additional salt, if desired.

4   If you are eating immediately, divide the salad between bowls or plates and serve warm, at room temperature, or chilled. If you are taking this to go, pack a serving of salad in a container. Seal and refrigerate it until you are ready to take it with you. Store your salad in the work refrigerator or with a cooler pack in your lunch bag until lunchtime.

✱ RESTYLE: MAKE IT A JAR MEAL
While the tossed salad can be added quickly to jars, you may want to flex your artistic muscle and turn this recipe into a layered lunch. To the bottom of large glass jar, add 2 teaspoons each of balsamic vinegar, olive oil, and tamari or soy sauce,

followed by ½ cup of beans, 1 cup of roasted vegetables, ½ cup of kale or chard, and ⅓ cup of cooked barley. Seal and refrigerate it until you are ready to take it with you. When you arrive at work, transfer it to the refrigerator or keep it chilled with a cooler pack. When you're ready for lunch, shake and eat in the jar, or transfer to a bowl to toss and eat.

Citrus, Shrimp, and Quinoa Salad

WITH FETA

Sicilian orange salads with black olives are a staple of mine in the winter when citrus is at its peak, but they certainly aren't a whole meal. This citrus salad, however, is satisfying complete, combining sharp grapefruit, clementine, and lime, along with shrimp, quinoa, and feta. If you don't like shrimp, skip it or use thin slices of medium-rare steak (page 240) instead.

SERVES 4   ⧗ 20 MINUTES   ⏱ 2 DAYS

2 cups water

1 cup uncooked quinoa

16 medium shrimp, peeled and deveined

2 Tbsp extra-virgin olive oil

½ tsp salt

⅛ tsp chipotle chili powder or smoked paprika

2 cold grapefruits, peeled and sliced into rounds or segmented

4 cold clementines, peeled and segmented

4 oz feta, crumbled

12 Moroccan dry-cured or kalamata olives, pitted and chopped

1 lime, sliced

1   Preheat the oven to 425°F. For the quinoa, to a medium saucepan, add the water and quinoa and bring to a boil. Reduce to a simmer, cover, and cook for 15 minutes. Remove from the heat and let sit, covered, for 5 minutes. Uncover, fluff with a fork, and transfer to a large bowl.

2   For the shrimp, on a large rimmed baking sheet, toss the shrimp with the oil, salt, and chipotle powder or smoked paprika. Roast for 7 to 10 minutes, or until the shrimp are bright pink. Add to the bowl with the quinoa, along with the grapefruit, clementine, feta, and olives. Gently toss to combine.

3   If you are eating immediately, divide the salad between plates or bowls, top with the lime slices, and serve. If you are taking this to go, add a portion of the salad to a container, top with some lime slices, seal, and refrigerate until you are ready to take it with you. When you get to work, keep it chilled in the refrigerator or with a cooler pack in your bag until lunchtime. To serve, season with lime and enjoy.

Chopped Thai Salad

WITH PEANUT SAUCE

Shred, dice, peel, whisk, and assemble. That's all it takes for this DIY Thai-inspired salad, and a simple switch of the presentation makes a typical lunch slaw seem entirely gourmet. Change the proteins, vegetables, and fruit for what appeals to you—just don't skip the sauce.

SERVES 4 TO 6 ⧖ 15 MINUTES ⏱ 2 DAYS FOR CHOPPED THAI SALAD (DRESSED); 1 WEEK FOR PEANUT SAUCE

CHOPPED THAI SALAD

4 cups shredded savoy cabbage

One 12 oz package extra-firm tofu, pressed and diced

1 head broccoli, steamed or raw, finely chopped

1 red bell pepper, seeded and diced

½ field or English cucumber, peeled and thinly sliced into half-moons

1 ripe mango, peeled, cored, and diced

1½ cups coarsely chopped fresh cilantro

2 tsp minced fresh red Thai chili

2 tsp sesame seeds

1 lime, cut into wedges

PEANUT SAUCE

⅓ cup natural peanut butter or favorite Nut Butter (page 237)

2 Tbsp lime juice

1 Tbsp white miso paste

1 Tbsp gluten-free tamari

1 tsp toasted sesame oil

2 tsp minced fresh ginger

1 clove garlic, minced

3–4 Tbsp water

1   For the salad, on a large salad platter or a large rimmed baking sheet, arrange the cabbage, tofu, broccoli, bell pepper, cucumber, mango, and cilantro. Garnish with chili, sesame seeds, and lime wedges.

2   For the peanut sauce, in a medium bowl, whisk together all the sauce ingredients except the water. Add the water, 1 tablespoon at a time, until the sauce is thin enough to drizzle but still thick. Pour it into a small serving bowl and nestle on the platter or baking sheet with the salad.

3   If you are eating immediately, have your guests build and dress their own salads at the table. Or, in a large bowl, toss all the salad ingredients except lime wedges with peanut sauce until fully combined, then transfer to a large platter or bowl and serve with lime wedges for seasoning. Store the dressed salad in an airtight container for up to 2 days. If you are taking this to go, mix together the salad and peanut sauce, then add a portion to a container along with a sprinkle of chili, some sesame seeds, and a lime wedge. Seal and refrigerate it until you are ready to take it with you. Keep it in the work refrigerator or tucked away with a cooler pack in your lunch bag until you are ready to season it with lime, and eat.

Take your salad to the next level. In a container, add a serving each of cooked rice (jasmine or basmati), salad tossed with peanut sauce, thinly sliced steak (page 240), chopped roasted peanuts, chili, sesame seeds, and a lime wedge. Keep it in the refrigerator or tucked away with a cooler pack in your lunch bag until you are ready to season it with fresh lime, and eat.

Butternut Squash Kale Salad

WITH ROASTED GARLIC DRESSING

I was in my early twenties when I "discovered" roasted vegetable salads. I would roast butternut squash, cherry tomatoes, and onion with olive oil, salt, and pepper, then toss it all with a handful of baby spinach and splash of vinegar. If I was lucky and had goat cheese in the refrigerator, I would crumble it over the works while everything was still warm. My techniques may now be more refined (I no longer put the oven on full blast, and make a proper dressing, for instance), but I still love that meal. This new yet familiar version of my old standby continues to satisfy me for lunch, but today, I'm using smarter lunch hacks with greens that get better as they sit instead of wilting down to nothing. A base of kale in place of spinach means I can make this salad ahead of time, as it can marinate for a few days, getting more flavorful with each passing hour.

SERVES 4   ⧗ 35 MINUTES   ⟳ 4 DAYS

1 butternut squash, peeled, seeded, and cut into ½-inch cubes

4 whole cloves garlic, skin intact

4 Tbsp extra-virgin olive oil, divided

½ tsp salt, divided

3 Tbsp apple cider vinegar

1 Tbsp Dijon mustard

1 tsp maple syrup

½ tsp dried thyme

Ground black pepper

1 bunch (8 cups) kale, de-stemmed and torn

½ cup grated parmesan

2 thick slices whole-grain sourdough or olive boule, well toasted and drizzled with olive oil

1   For the roasted squash and roasted garlic, preheat the oven to 400°F. On a large rimmed baking sheet, toss the squash and garlic with 1 tablespoon of oil and ¼ teaspoon of salt. Spread into an even layer. Roast for 30 to 35 minutes, until the squash is very tender and the garlic is soft. Set aside.

2   For the dressing, in a small bowl to whisk or a glass jar to shake, combine the remaining 3 tablespoons of oil and ¼ teaspoon of salt, vinegar, mustard, maple syrup, thyme, and pepper to taste. Squeeze the roasted garlic cloves out of their papers, discard the papers, and add them to the dressing. Whisk to combine or seal the jar and shake vigorously, until the mixture is mostly emulsified.

3   For the salad, in a large bowl, massage the kale with your hands until it is dark green and soft, about 1 minute. Add the squash, dressing, and half the cheese. Toss to combine, divide among plates or bowls, and tear over oiled bread. Serve warm, at room temperature, or chilled, with the remaining cheese sprinkled over top.

4   If you are taking this to go, add a portion of salad to your container. Pack the torn bread and remaining cheese separately or rest them on a piece of parchment paper placed on top of the salad. Seal and refrigerate until you are ready to take it with you. When you get to work, store it in the refrigerator or with a cooler pack in your lunch bag. To serve, top the salad with the torn bread and cheese, then enjoy.

Greek Chopped Salad

WITH CRISPY PEPPERCORN SALMON

Salmon is one of the only fish that tastes just as nice warm out of the pan as it does chilled. This chopped salad comes together in under 15 minutes and can be made year-round, tasting even better during prime tomato season, which runs from late August to early September. If you're crunched for time, swap the salmon for a cupful of chickpeas, pack it all up, and run out the door.

SERVES 4   ⏳ 15 MINUTES   ⏱ 1 DAY

GREEK CHOPPED SALAD

¼ cup extra-virgin olive oil

3 Tbsp red wine vinegar

1 pint cherry tomatoes, halved or quartered

1 English cucumber, unpeeled and diced

½ red onion, finely diced

1 Tbsp chopped fresh oregano

½ cup crumbled feta

10 kalamata olives, pitted and sliced

CRISPY PEPPERCORN SALMON

Four 4 oz skinless salmon fillets

Salt

1 Tbsp whole black peppercorns

2 Tbsp extra-virgin olive oil

1   For the salad, in a large bowl, add the oil (skip for now if packing), vinegar (skip for now if packing), tomatoes, cucumber, onion, and oregano. Toss to combine, then gently mix in the feta and olives. Set aside.

2   For the salmon, season the salmon with salt. With a mortar and pestle, crush the peppercorns to a medium-coarse texture. Coat one side of the salmon with peppercorns. Preheat a large cast-iron or nonstick skillet over medium-high heat and add the oil, followed by the salmon, peppercorn side down. Sear on the first side for 2 to 3 minutes, carefully flip (the fish will release when it is ready to flip), and cook on the second side until it reaches the desired doneness, about 2 to 3 minutes for juicy, medium-cooked salmon with a crispy crust.

3   If eating immediately, add the salad to plates or bowls, with the salmon on the side or on top, and serve. If taking to go, for each container, pack the oil and vinegar for the salad in a small container on the side (use 1 tablespoon of extra-virgin olive oil and ¾ tablespoon of red wine vinegar per person). Add a serving of undressed, mixed salad to a container along with a fillet of salmon. Alternatively, build in a jar, starting with the oil and vinegar dressing (as above), followed by a serving of undressed mixed salad, and finishing with the salmon fillet, flaked. Seal and refrigerate it until you are ready to take it with you. Keep it in the work refrigerator or with a cooler pack in your lunch bag until you are ready to eat. To serve, top the salad with oil and vinegar, mix, and eat, or shake the jar and eat.

Farro, Beet, Asparagus, and Watercress Picnic Salad

Picnic salads need to be movable, sturdy, and low on the frilly lettuces, which tend to wilt dangerously fast under the hot sun. Don't let the name dictate where to eat it, though—this meal packs well for lunch at work and looks handsome spread on a platter at home. The vegetables I use are spring-specific, but you can replace them with any similarly textured and sized produce seasonally available to you. As this salad sits, and especially if you make it a couple of days in advance, the salad becomes ludicrously magenta in color, and it's absolutely beautiful.

SERVES 4 TO 6   ⧗ 55 MINUTES   ⟳ 4 DAYS

3 large or 6 small beets

1 cup uncooked farro

½ pound asparagus, tough ends removed, cut into bite-sized pieces

1 large bunch (5–6 cups) coarsely chopped watercress

6 radishes, very thinly sliced

¼ cup toasted pine nuts

1 clove garlic, minced

¼ cup lemon juice

¼ cup extra-virgin olive oil

2 Tbsp balsamic vinegar

½ tsp salt

Ground black pepper

Shaved parmesan or crumbled goat cheese (optional), for serving

1   For the roasted beets, preheat the oven to 400°F. Wrap the unpeeled beets in foil and roast them for 45 minutes to 1 hour, or until they are tender when you jab them with a paring knife. Unwrap and allow them to cool until you can comfortably peel and quarter them, then add them to a large bowl.

2   For the farro, in a medium saucepan, cover the farro with 3 to 4 inches of water, bring to a boil, reduce the heat to medium-low, and simmer for 25 to 35 minutes, or until tender. Drain and rinse with cold water. Add to the large bowl with the beets.

3   For the asparagus, in a large wide skillet or high-sided saucepan, add a splash of water to the asparagus, cover, and steam until tender, about 4 minutes. Rinse with cold water and dry well. Add the asparagus to the beets and farro, along with the watercress, radishes, pine nuts, garlic, lemon juice, olive oil, balsamic vinegar, salt, and pepper to taste. Mix gently but thoroughly to combine the mixture without crushing the watercress. If not eating immediately, store in an airtight container in the refrigerator.

4   If you are eating the salad now, divide it among bowls, top it with the parmesan or goat cheese (if using), and serve. If taking the salad to go, pack it in a container and top with the parmesan or goat cheese (if using). Seal and refrigerate it until you are ready to take it with you. When you get to work, store it in the refrigerator or with a cooler pack in your lunch bag until you are ready to eat it.

Sunday Kale Salad

My insurance policy for getting my greens almost every day of the workweek is making a big batch of kale salad on Sunday that's dedicated strictly to lunches. Kale salads may seem unremarkable, basic, and overdone, but this one, layered with textures and flavors, sewn together with balsamic vinaigrette, is sure to become a staple in lunches at work, at play, at home, and on the fly. Any cooked protein, be it chicken, beans, or canned tuna or sardines, will boost this salad's staying power.

SERVES 4 AS A MAIN OR 6 AS A SIDE ⏳ 45 MINUTES
🕐 4 DAYS

1 For the salad, preheat the oven to 400°F. On a large rimmed baking sheet, toss the sweet potato with the oil and salt. Roast for 25 to 35 minutes, until the sweet potato is tender and beginning to brown. Remove from the oven and allow to cool slightly.

2 Add the kale to a large bowl and massage it with your hands until the leaves have darkened and tenderized, about 1 minute. Add the roasted sweet potatoes, walnuts or pecans, and dried cranberries. Toss with desired amount of vinaigrette. Store in an airtight container in the refrigerator for up to 4 days.

3 If you are eating immediately, serve the salad topped with, or next to, your protein of choice. If you are taking this to go, pack a serving of salad and your protein of choice in a container. Seal and refrigerate it until you are ready to take it with you. Keep the salad cold in your workplace refrigerator or in your lunch bag with a cooler pack until you're ready to eat.

★ SWAP ROASTED BEETS FOR THE SWEETS

Preheat the oven to 400°F. Wrap 4 unpeeled beets in foil and roast for 45 minutes to 1 hour, or until tender when pierced with a knife. Unwrap the foil and let the beets cool slightly, then peel and cube the beets, and add them to the salad along with some Pickled Red Onions (page 243).

1 large or 2 small sweet potatoes, peeled and cut into small cubes

1 Tbsp coconut oil or extra-virgin olive oil

¼ tsp salt

1 bunch kale, tough stems removed, shredded (about 8 cups)

½ cup chopped walnuts or pecans

¼ cup dried cranberries, chopped

Balsamic Vinaigrette, as needed (page 236)

4 servings protein of choice (chicken, tuna, chickpeas, hard-boiled eggs, steak, etc.)

Zucchini Tangle

WITH ROMESCO AND BURRATA

Romesco, a thick Spanish condiment with a similar texture to hummus, is made from roasted red peppers, nuts, and often smoked paprika. It is incredibly versatile, marrying with more than just zucchini noodles (find more ideas on page 134, in the Lunch Note). It's a sauce that can be made with any nut or seed you desire, including roasted almonds, hazelnuts, or, as I've used here, super-healthy hemp hearts.

SERVES 4 ⧗ 55 MINUTES ⏱ 1 WEEK FOR ROMESCO; 2 DAYS ASSEMBLED JAR MEAL (SEE LUNCH NOTE)

1 For the romesco, preheat the oven to 375°F. Line a large rimmed baking sheet with parchment paper and toss the peppers, onion, and garlic with 2 tablespoons of oil. Roast for 40 to 50 minutes, until the vegetables are soft and beginning to caramelize.

2 Transfer the vegetables to a food processor and pulse until finely chopped. Add the remaining 2 tablespoons of oil, hemp hearts, vinegar, paprika, and salt. Blend until smooth, scrape down the sides, and briefly blend again. If you are not using this immediately, refrigerate in an airtight container for up to 1 week or freeze for up to 3 months.

3 To serve, add the zucchini to a large bowl and toss with some romesco. Tear the burrata directly over the bowls (so you don't lose any of that creamy filling) or top with coarsely torn mozzarella, and add the oregano or basil. Enjoy chilled or at room temperature. See the Lunch Note for a packable option.

CONTINUED

ROMESCO

2 red bell peppers, seeded and coarsely chopped

2 onions coarsely chopped

2 whole cloves garlic, peeled

4 Tbsp extra-virgin olive oil, divided

¼ cup hulled hemp hearts or unsalted roasted almonds

2 Tbsp sherry vinegar or red wine vinegar

½ tsp smoked paprika

½ tsp salt

ZUCCHINI NOODLES AND BURRATA

2 medium zucchinis, spiral sliced or shaved

1 ball (8 oz) fresh burrata or fresh mozzarella

Fresh oregano leaves or fresh basil, torn, for garnish

★ RESTYLE: MAKE IT A JAR MEAL

For one serving, in the bottom of a large glass jar, add a large dollop of romesco, followed by a portion each of torn fresh mozzarella (burrata will be too messy for packing), shredded poached chicken (page 239), torn oregano or basil leaves, and zucchini noodles. Seal and refrigerate until you are ready to take it with you. Keep your jar chilled in the work refrigerator or with a cooler pack in your lunch bag until you are ready to shake it or toss it in a bowl, and eat.

★ MORE WITH ROMESCO

Romesco adds an alluring, smoky zip to just about any savory dish. Toss it with cold cooked brown rice, chickpeas, and fresh herbs for a hearty grain salad; pasta and steamed kale; or cooked white beans and tuna. Use it as a dip for roasted vegetables (fingerling potatoes are especially nice here) or spread it on toast before you pop on the avocado— the possibilities are plentiful.

Greens and Farro

WITH CHICKEN, AVOCADO, AND
HONEY-MUSTARD DRESSING

I've had many salad phases in my life. One summer of my childhood, bottled oil and vinegar dressing tossed with iceberg lettuce was my specialty. Then came salads slicked with a low-fat dressing, combining fruit, seeds, and spring mix lettuce. Fast-food salads came on the scene soon after. My order was a big (ready-made) bowl of crunchy lettuce, grated cheddar cheese, chicken, cucumber (that was always desiccated beyond repair), and the saving grace that made it work: honey-mustard dressing. The dressing was sharp, tangy, sweet, and creamy—the perfect complement for vegetables. My homemade version brings this nostalgic dressing home without the weird ingredients, pairing it with a salad base that speaks to my current palate and riper age.

SERVES 4 ⧗ 45 MINUTES ⟳ 3 DAYS

1 For the dressing, in a small bowl, whisk the Dijon, oil, vinegar, honey, salt, and garlic until creamy. Set aside.

2 Preheat a grill or grill pan to medium-high heat.

3 For the farro, in a medium saucepan, add the farro and cover with 2 inches of water. Bring to a boil, reduce the heat to medium-low, and cook partially covered for 25 to 30 minutes, until the grains are tender and beginning to burst. Drain well and add to a large high-sided skillet. Add half the dressing to the farro along with the greens and sauté over medium heat until the greens are dark green and wilted, about 1 minute.

4 For the chicken, lightly grease the chicken with oil and season with salt and pepper. Grill for 5 to 6 minutes per side, until the juices run clear and grill marks are visible. The thickest part of the chicken should read 160°F to 165°F on an instant-read thermometer. Allow to rest for at least 5 minutes before slicing. Set aside.

CONTINUED

HONEY-MUSTARD DRESSING

¼ cup Dijon mustard

¼ cup extra-virgin olive oil

¼ cup apple cider vinegar

2 Tbsp honey

½ tsp salt

¼ clove garlic, grated

FARRO, GREENS, AND GRILLED CHICKEN

½ cup uncooked farro

1 bunch kale or dandelion greens or other sturdy greens, tough stems removed, coarsely chopped

Two 8 oz boneless, skinless chicken breasts

Extra-virgin olive oil, for greasing

Salt

Ground black pepper

2 avocados

5 If you are eating immediately, halve, pit, and peel the avocados. Add the farro and greens mixture to serving plates, then top with avocado halves (1 half per person) and sliced chicken. Drizzle with more dressing to taste (you'll likely have leftovers) and serve warm, at room temperature, or chilled. If you are taking this to go, pack a portion each of the farro and greens mixture, the avocado, and the chicken in a container, and drizzle the avocado with additional dressing to keep it from browning. Seal and refrigerate until you are ready to take it with you. Keep the salad chilled in the work refrigerator or with a cooler pack until it's time for lunch.

Lemony Barley and Roasted Carrot Salad

WITH GOAT CHEESE

4 medium carrots, peeled
   and cut into ½-inch
   rounds

3 Tbsp extra-virgin olive oil,
   divided

Salt

1 cup uncooked pearl barley

¼ cup lemon juice

2 tsp dried mint

¼–½ clove garlic, minced

Ground black pepper

1 cup chopped fresh cilantro
   or parsley, a spoonful
   reserved for garnish

½ cup pomegranate seeds,
   a few reserved for
   garnish

4 oz fresh goat cheese,
   broken

★ PERKED UP

Grain salads, like this
one, often need a lift
with something acidic
after a couple of days of
refrigeration. To perk up
grain salads that have
fallen flat, before serving,
top them with a squeeze
of lemon or dribble of
vinegar, and, optionally, a
bit of olive oil and salt.
This trick works for
virtually any grain to
make the dish feel
freshly made.

Lemon juice, olive oil, and mint bring zest to this chewy grain salad. Pomegranate seeds add crunch, juice, and sweetness, while carrots ground the dish with their earthiness. A goat cheese snowcap on top makes this simple salad noteworthy.

SERVES 4   ☒ 30 MINUTES   ⏱ 3 DAYS

1   For the salad, preheat the oven to 400°F. On a large rimmed baking sheet, toss the carrots with 1 tablespoon of oil and season with salt. Roast for 20 to 25 minutes, until tender and caramelized on the bottom. Set aside.

2   Meanwhile, in a medium saucepan, cover the barley with 4 inches of water. Bring to a boil, reduce to a simmer, partially cover, and cook for 25 minutes, or until the barley is tender. Drain, rinse with cold water, and drain again.

3   Add the barley to a large bowl along with the lemon juice, remaining 2 tablespoons of olive oil, mint, garlic, and salt and pepper to taste. Add the cooked carrots, cilantro or parsley, and pomegranate seeds to the barley mixture and toss well.

4   If you are eating immediately, add the salad to serving bowls or plates and top it with the goat cheese and the reserved cilantro or parsley and pomegranate seeds. Serve warm, at room temperature, or chilled. If you are taking this to go, pack your desired serving of salad in a container and top it with goat cheese and the reserved cilantro or parsley and pomegranate seeds. Seal and refrigerate it until you are ready to take it with you. Refrigerate the salad again when you arrive at work or keep it chilled with a cooler pack until lunchtime.

PART III

SHARING LUNCH ON THE WEEKEND

(modern midday hosting)

THIS SECTION BEGINS by celebrating one of the heroes of shareable entertaining, midday on a Saturday or Sunday: the platter. Gather, assemble, and add as few or as many homemade touches as you love. Pull inspiration from what's in season, available, or notable to you. Turn to your local farmers' market or a grocery store with a variety of deli items, and take your collection to the next level with a twist of the wrist and a bit of platter assembly know-how.

Brunch, which is any time during the many midday hours on a weekend, often overlaps with or replaces lunch, making its inclusion in this cookbook mandatory. While brunch in North America tends to begin as early as 10 a.m., elsewhere, I've seen brunch start at 2 p.m., if not 3 p.m. (I cannot wait that long to eat my first meal(!), so I like having it somewhere in the middle.) It's the perfect meal to share with pals—nearly everyone I've met loves brunch food, and it's really impossible to not have a good time when coffee and possibly cocktails are being served.

No guests? No problem. Don't be shy about treating yourself and maybe a partner or friend to a weekend meal with meaning. If you have kids, get them in on these awesome weekend lunches, too.

If you're a weekend adventurer, pack a picnic, attend or create an event, and soak in a change of scenery. Pick a theme, plan a menu around it, and prepare the food based on that. Whether you put a mountain of preparation into the meal or start packing with very little forethought, getting away from the usual setting for a change of scenery makes any dish taste really, really good.

Of course, I need to mention the best part of modern midday hosting: early afternoon entertaining on the weekend means that you have all of the late afternoon and evening to spend as you choose. Close—or start—the week with a bang.

CHAPTER 6

Platters

I CANNOT TELL YOU how many times a platter has saved me. My partner, Geoff, and I enjoy hosting parties, and platters are our go-to. It's then when I turn to my Gathered Platter (page 145), meaning that I take all the help I can get from locally made breads, the cheese shop, and the deli bar, where I can buy several varieties of olives and pickles and supplement it all with a homemade dip or two. Now that we live abroad, there's no better way to make new friends than by inviting them over for weekend lunch, especially when that lunch includes a platter of curated bites from around the city. The more people, the more I recommend that you shouldn't make everything yourself. Have some fun at lunchtime, I say!

Punctuate your platter with something cool to drink, and ask a friend to bring along some cookies or a couple of bars of dark chocolate. If you treat entertaining on a weekend day as work, then you won't do it. Platters do the work for you, coaxing out conversation while guests build their own meal—a win-win for weekend entertaining.

A Gathered Platter

Adaptable for any crowd size, budget, time constraint, craving, and locale. Shop the farmers' market in the spring and summer, local small-batch shops in the winter, or a combination of both year-round. If time allows and you have the ambition, make more of the components from scratch. Practice your weekday lunchtime rituals on the weekend, and be smart with your time in the kitchen. Gather, cook as much or as little as you like, assemble, eat, and enjoy your efforts and company.

SERVES 6   ⧗ 45 MINUTES   ⟳ 1 WEEK FOR ROASTED RED PEPPER FETA DIP

1   For the dip, preheat the oven to 400°F. Line a large rimmed baking sheet with parchment paper. Place peppers cut side down and add garlic to tray. Roast until peppers are mostly blackened on the exterior and beginning to collapse, about 30 minutes. When cool enough to handle, peel off most of the blackened pepper skin and all of the garlic skin; add both to a food processor along with the feta or goat cheese, olive oil, vinegar, salt, and chili flakes and blend until smooth. Store in an airtight container in the refrigerator for up to 1 week.

2   To assemble the platter, place the roasted red pepper dip and hummus or baba ghanoush (if using) in a serving bowl. Arrange remaining components on a platter, in small bowls, or scattered on a clean tablecloth. Guests can help themselves, building a personalized lunch to linger over with drinks.

ROASTED RED PEPPER FETA DIP

2 red peppers, halved and seeded

2 whole cloves garlic, skin intact

6 oz feta or goat cheese

1 Tbsp extra-virgin olive oil

1 Tbsp red wine vinegar

½ tsp salt

Red chili flakes

PLATTER

1 recipe Roasted Red Pepper Feta Dip (above)

1 cup prepared or homemade hummus or baba ghanoush (optional)

2–3 cheeses, a mixture of hard and soft varieties

12 oz cured meat and/or cured fish (salami, prosciutto, gravlax, etc.)

1 lb small fresh fruit (clementines, grapes, sliced apples, cherries, etc.)

1 cup dried fruit (dates, cranberries, figs, apricots, etc.)

1 cup assorted olives and pickled vegetables

½ cup red currant jelly or fruit preserves of choice

¼ cup honey or 1 sheet of honeycomb

1 fresh baguette, sliced

1 package (6½ oz) whole-grain crackers

Meze

Many years ago, on a trip to London, England, with my dad, I had my first meze, a platter-style arrangement of small dishes hailing from former Ottoman Empire countries. A very-early-twenties me and my dad sat on the patio of a restaurant on the River Thames, enjoying salty, jet lag–curing nibbles of this and that from Lebanon, Greece, Turkey, Georgia, and more. It's a beautiful way to present lunch, be it platter-style abroad or at home, or container-style at work. Think of meze as a many-course lunch presented in one go, which guests can pick away at, build a plate with, or use to build a full-on falafel-stuffed pita.

SERVES 4 TO 6 ⧖ 30 MINUTES PLUS 12 HOURS FOR FALAFEL (PAGE 65) ⟳ 1 WEEK FOR ALL

1 For the hummus, in a food processor, pulse the garlic until minced. Add the lemon juice and blend for a few seconds. Let the garlic sit in the lemon juice for 10 minutes to mellow its sharpness. Add the tahini, ¼ cup chickpea can liquid or water, the cumin, and the salt. Blend until fluffy and whipped. Add the chickpeas and blend. Scrape down the sides and blend again for 2 to 3 minutes until soft and creamy. If the mixture is too thick, add additional chickpea can liquid or water, 1 tablespoon at a time, blending between additions, until the hummus has the desired consistency. Store in an airtight container in the refrigerator until you are ready to use it. Bring to room temperature before serving, for the best flavor.

2 For the whipped feta, in a food processor, pulse the feta until finely crumbled. Add the yogurt and pulse to combine. Scrape down the sides and blend for about 30 seconds, until the mixture is creamy. If you are not using it immediately, store it in an airtight container in the refrigerator.

3 For the salad, in a large bowl, toss together all the salad ingredients except anchovies until combined. Transfer to a serving bowl and top with the anchovies (if using).

CONTINUED

HUMMUS

2 cloves garlic

¼ cup lemon juice

⅓ cup tahini

One 19 oz can chickpeas, can liquid and 1 Tbsp whole chickpeas reserved

½ tsp ground cumin

½ tsp salt

WHIPPED FETA

10½ oz feta

6 Tbsp plain Greek yogurt, preferably whole milk

TOMATO-CUCUMBER CHOPPED SALAD

2 beefsteak tomatoes, diced

2 cups diced unpeeled English cucumber or peeled and seeded field cucumber

1 cup thinly sliced red onion

2 Tbsp extra-virgin olive oil

1 Tbsp red wine vinegar or white wine vinegar

2 tsp pomegranate molasses

¼ tsp salt

8 whole anchovies packed in olive oil (optional)

PLATTER

1 recipe Falafel (page 65)

4–6 Pita or flatbread

1 Tbsp extra-virgin olive oil

Red chili flakes

Pinch of powdered dried hibiscus or sumac

¼ cup fresh mint leaves, coarsely chopped if large

1 head red leaf lettuce or baby romaine, leaves separated

1 cup olives of choice

4   To assemble the platter, warm the falafel and the pita or flatbread in a 300°F oven for 5 to 8 minutes (these will dry out if left too long), or warm the pita or flatbread in the oven and shallow-fry the falafel in vegetable oil until crispy (I prefer the shallow-fry).

5   Swirl the hummus into a large shallow serving bowl, drizzle it with the olive oil, and top with the reserved 1 tablespoon of chickpeas and the red chili flakes to taste. Swirl the whipped feta onto a plate and sprinkle lightly with the hibiscus or sumac. Scatter the mint leaves over the hummus and whipped feta. Surround the hummus and whipped feta with the warmed falafel and pita, salad, lettuce leaves, and olives. Serve with plates for guests to make their own unique dish.

* RESTYLE: PACKED LUNCH

A sectioned lunch container can transport a mini meze to work, the beach, the park, and beyond.

* RESTYLE: MEZE 2

Surround homemade or prepared hummus, topped with olive oil and dukkah (page 168) or sesame seeds, with homemade or prepared falafel, jarred roasted red peppers, cubes of feta tossed with fresh herbs, cucumber, baby romaine leaves, olives, and pita. Garnish with oregano sprigs and serve.

Easygoing Lunchtime Platter Ideas

Shop, prep, and assemble a spread that will delight a lunchtime crowd of any size. Here are some platter concept combos to get you started.

· goat brie + blackberries + plums + salami + Marcona almonds

· steamed new potatoes + hard-boiled eggs + steamed shrimp + blanched green beans + blanched asparagus + baby tomatoes + gem lettuce + radicchio + radishes (or any combination of cooked and raw vegetables you like) + aioli

· hummus (page 147) + crudités + cherry tomatoes + pita

· manchego + seeded breads + prosciutto + cantaloupe + walnuts + honey + gherkins

· sharp white cheddar + toasted baguette + honey + peaches + walnuts

· smoked mackerel + steamed new potatoes + cucumber + sourdough + aioli + cultured butter

· goat cheese + roasted beets + aged balsamic vinegar + baguette + roasted hazelnuts

· blue cheese + cornichons + Pickled Red Onions (page 243) + dried apples + fruit and nut crackers

· steamed asparagus + French Vinaigrette (page 236) + hard-boiled eggs + smoked salmon + sesame bagels + cream cheese + capers

· crostini + toppings of choice (roasted tomatoes, cheeses, cured meats, pesto, etc.)

· blue brie + sourdough baguette + honeycomb + pears + capocollo + cocktail tomatoes

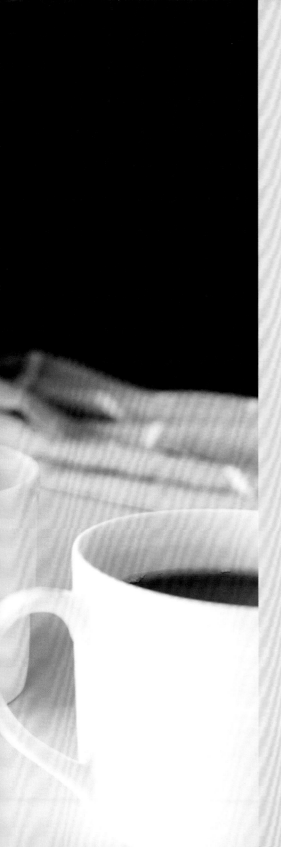

CHAPTER 7

Brunch for Lunch

BREAKFAST FOR DINNER is something I do often, so why not breakfast for lunch? Or better yet, brunch for lunch?

Many of the following brunch for lunch recipes stand on their own as meals, but brunchtime itself is time for a spread. Make them all at once for a super-brunch (hats off to you!) or only one, pairing your pick with any number of salads, sliced fresh citrus fruit, berries, bacon, toast, and preserves.

For me, breakfast should be extremely healthy. And most mornings, I prefer a sweeter start—usually plain yogurt with granola and fruit or homemade muesli and fruit. But brunch is a time to eat sturdier, more savory fare. Regardless of the healthfulness of the ingredients, brunch just feels indulgent. I propose it's the time we take to prepare and craft a brunch that feels decadent, as well as the slower pace at which we eat it. We take the time to make coffee (a recipe for the best pour-over coffee awaits you) and, perhaps, a cocktail. Skip the restaurant queue and make brunch for lunch a new tradition whenever time allows.

Savory Avocado French Toast

Hold the maple syrup and rethink classic, sweet-leaning French toast. Instead, thick, rustic sourdough is soaked in an egg batter, then fried, creating a crisp yet tender French toast base to cover with ripe, buttery avocado, herby chimichurri, salty feta, and juicy tomatoes. I like to use day-old bread for the French toast as it soaks up the egg batter more efficiently, leading to a custardy interior and crispy exterior. For a real weekend friend feast, supply all of the toppings on the table for everyone to decorate as they see fit.

SERVES 4   ⏲ 25 MINUTES   ⏱ 1 WEEK

CHIMICHURRI

1 bunch fresh cilantro with tender stems, coarsely chopped

1 clove garlic

1 green chili or 1 jalapeño, coarsely chopped (remove seeds for milder sauce)

¼ tsp salt

2 Tbsp apple cider vinegar or lime juice

1 tsp Worcestershire sauce (gluten-free and/or vegan, if desired)

⅓ cup extra-virgin olive oil, more as needed

FRENCH TOAST AND TOPPINGS

4 large eggs

½ cup milk of choice

¾ tsp salt, plus more for serving

4 slices sourdough or rustic bread of choice (preferably day-old), thickly sliced

2 Tbsp extra-virgin olive oil or salted butter, plus more olive oil for serving

2 large ripe avocados, room temperature, halved, pitted, peeled, and thinly sliced

1 pint cherry tomatoes, halved

Crumbled feta, for garnish

Sunflower sprouts, for garnish

1   For the chimichurri, in a food processor, pulse the cilantro, garlic, chili or jalapeño, and salt until finely minced. Blend in the vinegar or lime juice and Worcestershire sauce. With the machine running, drizzle in the oil through the top chute until a slick dressing forms. It should be slightly runny; if it's too paste-like, add additional oil until it falls off the spoon. Store in an airtight container in the refrigerator until you are ready to use it.

2   For the French toast, preheat the oven to 300°F to warm the serving plates and keep the fried French toast hot. In a 9- × 13-inch glass baking dish, whisk the eggs, milk, and salt until fully combined. Add the bread to the egg mixture, turning to coat. Allow the bread to soak in the liquid for 10 minutes, flipping once or twice. In a large cast-iron or nonstick skillet, heat the oil or butter over medium heat. Add the soaked bread in a single layer, cooking in batches if necessary to avoid overcrowding. Cook for 3 to 4 minutes on the first side, until golden brown on the bottom; flip and cook for 3 to 4 minutes longer on the second side, until golden brown on the bottom. Keep warm on a baking sheet in the oven if cooking in batches.

3   To serve, add French toast to warmed serving plates and top with avocado, tomatoes, feta, chimichurri, sprouts, a drizzle of additional oil, and an extra pinch of salt.

★ FRENCH TOAST + AVOCADO +

· smoked salmon + lemon + yogurt

· cooked lentils + manchego + pesto

· Greek yogurt + fresh blackberries

· hummus + roasted red peppers

· blueberry jam + bacon

· tapenade + sardines + lemon

· fried egg + bacon + tomato jam

Saag-Style Eggs

WITH PRESERVED LEMON

This is the recipe I want to eat every day, inspired by saag paneer, a rich, addictive Indian dish made with any number of greens—usually spinach—lashed with cream, smudged with spices, and dotted with paneer, a fresh milk cheese. I've taken the idea, choosing eggs over paneer and cashew "cream" (you could use 1 cup canned coconut milk) for cream, making this a shakshuka-saag hybrid that fills your home with a heady aroma, and your belly with good-quality protein and greens.

SERVES 4   ⧖ 45 MINUTES   ⧗ 3 DAYS FOR SAAG (WITHOUT EGGS)

CASHEW CREAM

(or use 1 cup canned coconut milk)

½ cup unsalted raw cashews

⅔ cup recently boiled water

SAAG

¼ cup coconut oil

4 cloves garlic, minced

1 serrano chili, finely minced (use less or more depending on heat level desired)

1 Tbsp finely grated fresh ginger

1 Tbsp garam masala

1 tsp ground cumin

1 tsp turmeric

1 tsp salt

Ground black pepper

1½ lb (2 bunches) spinach, very well washed and dried, finely chopped

1 Tbsp lemon juice

4–8 large eggs, depending on hunger levels

¼ cup finely chopped fresh cilantro

2 Tbsp diced preserved lemon, skin only, or 1 tsp grated lemon zest

2 cups cooked basmati rice, for serving (optional)

4 naan, for serving (optional)

½ cup plain yogurt, for serving (optional)

1   Preheat the oven to 350°F. To make the cashew cream, add the cashews and recently boiled water to a blender, cover, and set aside for 10 minutes. Blend on high until smooth and creamy. Set aside.

2   For the saag, heat the coconut oil over medium heat in a large oven-safe high-sided or cast-iron skillet. Add the garlic, chili, ginger, garam masala, cumin, turmeric, salt, and pepper to taste; sauté until fragrant and sizzling, about 30 seconds. Add the spinach in two parts, cooking until wilted after each addition. Stir in the prepared cashew cream and lemon juice, and remove from the heat. Optionally, you can now puree this spinach mixture in a blender or food processor if you'd like an ultra-creamy saag.

3   Make small dents in the top of the saag for the eggs to rest in, and crack in the eggs. Bake for 15 to 20 minutes, until the egg whites are set but the yolks are still slightly runny. Garnish with cilantro and preserved lemon or lemon zest. Serve with rice, naan, and yogurt, if desired.

★ MAKE-AHEAD

Prepare the entire recipe without adding the eggs, up to 3 days in advance, and store it in an airtight container in the refrigerator. On the day of, bring it to room temperature, crack in the eggs, and bake according to the directions.

Polenta Porridge

WITH BROCCOLI RABE, TOMATOES, AND EGGS

Porridge needn't only be made with oats, nor does it need to be sweet. Serve this savory take for brunch or lunch when you have little time, few groceries, and a handful of guests. An almost-instant-gratification, feel-good, midday meal.

SERVES 4 ⏳ 15 MINUTES

POLENTA PORRIDGE

4–5 cups water or low-sodium vegetable broth

1 cup instant polenta

1 tsp salt

Ground black pepper

2 Tbsp salted butter

BROCCOLI RABE, TOMATOES, AND EGGS

2 Tbsp extra-virgin olive oil, plus more for cooking eggs and serving

1 pint cherry tomatoes

4 cloves garlic, smashed, kept whole

1 bunch broccoli rabe (rapini), tough ends trimmed, coarsely chopped

Salt

2 tsp red wine vinegar

4 large eggs

1 For the porridge, in a large pot, whisk 4 cups of water or broth with the polenta, salt, and pepper to taste. Whisking constantly, bring the mixture to a boil, reduce the heat to lowest level, cover, and cook, whisking a few times, for 8 to 10 minutes. Whisk in up to 1 cup of additional water if you prefer a thinner consistency. Whisk in the butter and keep warm, covered, over the lowest heat.

2 For the broccoli rabe, tomatoes, and eggs, in a large cast-iron or high-sided skillet, heat the oil over medium-high heat. Add the tomatoes and cook until they are blistered on the bottom side, about 5 to 8 minutes. Add the garlic and sauté until browned, about 1 minute. Add the broccoli rabe, reduce the heat to medium-low, and sauté until wilted, about 1 to 2 minutes. Season with salt to taste and the vinegar. Transfer to a large plate and cover to keep warm while you cook the eggs.

3 In the vegetable pan (no need to clean it), add a touch more oil to coat the bottom. Fry the eggs in the hot pan until they reach your desired doneness.

4 To serve, add the polenta porridge to shallow serving bowls and top it with vegetables, fried eggs, a drizzle of olive oil and a crack of pepper.

★ CLEAN SLATE

This grain porridge is a blank canvas that is eagerly awaiting leftover roasted vegetables, pesto, tomato sauce, baked fruit, yogurt, beans, bacon, and/or soft goat cheese. Choose your favorites, or simply use what you have on hand.

Rustic Spelt Quiche

WITH ASPARAGUS AND NEW POTATOES

Most quiche has a fluffy, custardy interior with a delicate, melt-in-your-mouth pastry shell. This quiche is sturdier, more packable, and can even be hand-held while eating, making it a really awesome picnic addition. Make it ahead and reheat it briefly in a low oven or serve it at room temperature, or even chilled: it's great all ways. For a special-occasion brunch or lunch, round out the meal with a cup of green pea and mint soup, a green salad, a basket of croissants with jam and butter, and a tray of dark chocolate brownies.

SERVES 4 AS A MAIN OR 6 AS A SIDE ⏳ 2 HOURS
🕁 3 DAYS

1   For the crust, in a food processor or by hand in a large bowl, pulse or cut the butter a few times to break up. Add flours, salt, and sugar and pulse or cut until only pea-sized pieces of butter remain. Add the ice water and pulse until a ball of dough forms.

2   Sprinkle additional flour on a clean surface. Roll the dough into a large circle approximately 11 to 13 inches in diameter, add to a 7- to 9-inch removable-bottom tart tin, then form the dough snuggly to the pan, allowing the sides to drape over a bit, if you like (or trim for a tidier look). Freeze until solid, about 30 minutes. If you making this ahead, once frozen, wrap the tin tightly in plastic, then foil, and freeze for up 3 months; bake from frozen (see next step) to prevent the dough from shrinking.

3   To blind bake the crust, preheat the oven to 425°F. Poke the bottom of the crust several times with a fork to allow steam to escape. Place a piece of parchment paper inside the crust, leaving overhang, and use a glass or ceramic pie plate that fits inside the tart tin or fill it with pie weights to weigh the crust down while it bakes. Bake for 15 minutes, remove the pie plate or weights and parchment paper, and bake for another 3 to 5 minutes, until the crust is dry on top and blond in color. Cool completely.

CONTINUED

SPELT CRUST

- ½ cup very cold unsalted butter, cut into small pieces
- ¾ cup unbleached all-purpose flour
- ½ cup light or dark spelt flour, plus more for rolling
- ¾ tsp salt
- ½ tsp granulated sugar
- ¼ cup ice water

FILLING

- ½ lb (2 small) new potatoes, sliced into 1/16 to 1/8-inch rounds
- 1 onion, sliced into 1/8-inch rounds
- ½ lb asparagus, tough ends trimmed, halved
- 1 Tbsp Dijon mustard
- 5 large eggs
- 1 cup whole milk or unsweetened non-dairy milk
- ½ tsp lemon zest (optional)
- ½ tsp dried thyme
- ½ tsp salt
- Ground black pepper

4   For the filling, bring a large pot of water to a boil. Blanch the potatoes and onion for 8 to 10 minutes, until they are still very firm but partially cooked; remove from the water and arrange on a large baking sheet to cool. Blanch the asparagus for 2 to 3 minutes, until it is bright green and just tender; remove it from the water and arrange it on a second large baking sheet or plate to cool.

5   Preheat the oven to 325°F. Brush the inside bottom of the cooled tart shell with the mustard and layer in the blanched and cooled vegetables, beginning with the potatoes, then the onion, and finishing with the asparagus.

6   In a medium bowl, whisk the eggs, milk, lemon zest (if using), thyme, and salt, and season with pepper. Slowly pour over the vegetables. Bake for 40 to 45 minutes, until the mixture still jiggles a little when tapped, but the eggs are set and dry on top. Cover loosely with a piece of parchment paper if the edges brown too quickly. Cool in the pan for 5 minutes.

7   To serve, carefully remove the quiche from the tart tin, slice into wedges, and enjoy warm, at room temperature, or chilled. Once cool, you can pack a slice to go in parchment paper or foil and reheat before enjoying, or eat it cold.

★ **MAKE-AHEAD**

Skip the last-minute brunch preparation, and the last-minute mess, and bake your quiche ahead of time. Once baked, cool, lightly cover, and refrigerate for up to 3 days. Enjoy a wedge packed to go or at home, cold or at room temperature, or reheat the entire quiche—or just a slice—in a 325°F oven until just warmed through, about 10 to 15 minutes.

Miso-Butter Mushrooms and Greens Toast

Steak-like with its deeply umami fragrance, texture, and taste, mushrooms on toast gets a mini makeover here, with a salty-sweet-tangy miso butter instead of the usual stodgy cream sauce.

For something lighter and naturally gluten-free, you can skip the bread and serve your toppings on a bed of steamed in-season asparagus, or even a piece of broiled salmon.

SERVES 4 ⏳ 15 MINUTES

1   For the mushrooms, greens, and eggs, in a large nonstick or cast-iron skillet, whisk the water, butter, miso, and vinegar over medium heat until the butter is melted and the mixture is emulsified and bubbling. Add the mushrooms in a single layer and cook on the first side for 3 to 4 minutes, or until golden brown; flip and cook for another 3 to 4 minutes, until golden brown on the second side. Transfer to a plate and cover to keep warm. Leave the pan on the heat and cook the greens until they are wilted and dark green, about 2 minutes; transfer them to the plate with the mushrooms. Add a touch more butter to the pan and fry the eggs as you like them.

2   To assemble the toast, drizzle the toasted bread with the olive oil, spread with mustard, and top with the greens, mushrooms, and fried eggs. Serve with avocado and season everything with salt, pepper, and chili flakes to taste.

★ **RESTYLE: ODE TO CREAMED MUSHROOMS ON TOAST**
Classics are classics for a reason: they work. If you crave a touch of cream with your mushrooms, skip the mustard and spread your toast with fresh goat cheese.

MISO-BUTTER MUSHROOMS, GREENS, AND EGGS

⅓ cup water

¼ cup unsalted butter, plus more for eggs

¼ cup white miso paste

1 Tbsp rice vinegar

4 cups cremini mushrooms, quartered

¾ lb baby kale or tender greens of choice, washed well, drained, and coarsely chopped

4 large eggs

TOAST AND TOPPINGS

4 slices sourdough or rustic bread of choice, thickly sliced and freshly toasted

Extra-virgin olive oil

Dijon mustard

2 avocados, peeled, pitted, and thinly sliced

Flaky salt

Ground black pepper

Red chili flakes

Even More Modern Ways with Toast

Finish savory combinations with a drizzle of olive oil and sprinkle of salt.

· toasted spouted grain bread + Hummus (page 147) + sauerkraut + Pickled Red Onions (page 243) + hard-boiled egg + parsley

· toasted sourdough + sliced peaches + griddled halloumi + mint + toasted pine nuts

· toasted split baguette + Whipped Feta (page 147) + heirloom tomatoes + smoked black pepper

· toasted seed and nuts bread + avocado + grapefruit segments + sprouts + black pepper

· toasted rye + miso-spiked Greek yogurt + sliced roasted beets + Pickled Red Onions (page 243)

· toasted sesame bagel + smashed avocado with lime + charred corn + crumbled queso fresco + hot sauce

· toasted sourdough rubbed with garlic + shaved serrano ham + cantaloupe chunks + black pepper

· toasted multigrain sourdough + butter + poached egg + feta + tomato + arugula + sumac + lemon

· toasted walnut bread + ricotta or labneh (page 72) + good-quality fruit preserves + chopped pistachios

Turkish Poached Eggs

WITH EGGPLANT ON SOCCA CREPES

When I need a quick, neutral, flavor-sopping base for bright-eyed taste, like Turkish poached eggs (cilbir), I turn to socca, a chickpea flour pancake. This colorful plate comes together in under 30 minutes, but I'll push you to take the extra few moments to really savor it at the table.

SERVES 4   ⏲ 20 MINUTES   ⏱ 5 DAYS FOR HERBED YOGURT; 2 DAYS FOR SOCCA

EGGPLANT

2 Tbsp extra-virgin olive oil

4 small or 2 large Chinese eggplants, cut into very thin rounds

¼ tsp salt

SOCCA

½ cup chickpea flour

½ cup water

¼ tsp salt

1 Tbsp extra-virgin olive oil

POACHED EGGS

1 Tbsp distilled white vinegar

4 large eggs

HERBED YOGURT AND SMOKED PAPRIKA OIL

⅔ cup plain Greek yogurt, preferably whole milk

½ cup finely chopped fresh cilantro or dill or a mixture, plus more for serving

1 Tbsp lemon juice

¼–½ clove garlic, minced

¼ tsp salt

2 Tbsp extra-virgin olive oil

½ tsp smoked paprika

Minced fresh red Thai chili

1   For the eggplant, heat the oil in a large nonstick skillet over medium heat. Once the oil is hot and shimmering, add the eggplant, sprinkle with the salt, and sear on first side for 2 to 3 minutes, until golden brown. Flip and continue to cook until golden brown on the second side, about 2 minutes. Transfer to a plate and cover. Set aside. Wipe the pan clean with a paper towel.

2   For the socca, in a medium bowl, whisk the chickpea flour, water, and salt until combined. In the wiped-clean large nonstick skillet, heat the oil over medium heat. Cooking one crepe at a time, add one-quarter of the socca batter to the pan and swirl until it is crepe-thin. Cook for 1 to 2 minutes, until completely dry on top and mostly golden brown on the bottom. No need to flip it; just transfer to a serving plate. Continue with the remaining socca batter. Set aside. Once cool, store the crepes in an airtight container at room temperature for up to 2 days.

3   For the poached eggs, fill a large high-sided skillet or the same nonstick skillet two-thirds full of tap water and add the vinegar. Bring to a gentle boil, crack in the eggs, remove from the heat, cover, and let sit for 6 minutes.

4   For the herbed yogurt and smoked paprika oil, in a medium bowl, mix the yogurt with the cilantro or dill, lemon juice, garlic, and salt until combined. Refrigerate in an airtight container for up to 5 days. In a small bowl, mix the oil with the smoked paprika until combined.

5   To serve, spread each socca crepe with herbed yogurt and top with eggplant. Using a slotted spoon, remove the eggs from the water, draining as much water as possible. Place on top of the eggplant, drizzle with smoked paprika oil, and sprinkle with additional herbs and Thai chili to taste.

Maple, Lemon, and Ginger Granola

Present this granola in a big bowl or glass jar with a scoop alongside yogurt and fruit, not forgetting to have the mini side bowls or glass jars at the ready. Or serve it up as a healthy snack during your weekday lunch.

MAKES APPROXIMATELY 6 CUPS ⏳ 1 HOUR 15 MINUTES
🕐 1 MONTH

1   Preheat the oven to 300°F. Line a large rimmed baking sheet with parchment paper.

2   In a large bowl, combine the oats, walnuts, almonds, ginger, and salt.

3   In a medium bowl, combine the maple syrup, coconut oil, lemon zest, vanilla, and orange flower water (if using). Add the maple syrup mixture to the oat mixture and stir thoroughly to coat.

4   Spread the granola onto the prepared baking sheet, pressing it loosely into a single layer. Bake for 55 minutes to 1 hour 5 minutes (no stirring), until it is uniformly golden and fragrant. Without stirring, let the granola cool completely on the baking sheet, to help larger, delicious granola clusters form naturally. Break up the fully cooled granola into your preferred size clusters, and store in an airtight container at room temperature for 1 to 2 months.

⭐ **RESTYLE: MAPLE, LEMON, AND GINGER GRANOLA PARFAITS**
Stir a touch of lemon zest and maple syrup, to taste, into thick, plain Greek yogurt. Spoon this mixture into small glasses or jars, and top it with berries and a scoop of this granola. Make these quickly before brunch guests arrive and put one down at each place setting. Or, if you're packing to go, keep the yogurt mixture, berries, and granola separated until you're ready to serve.

4 cups large-flake rolled oats

1 cup walnuts, chopped

½ cup almonds, chopped

1 tsp ground dried ginger

¾ tsp salt

½ cup maple syrup

⅓ cup coconut oil, melted

Zest of 1 lemon

½ tsp vanilla extract

¼ tsp orange flower water (optional)

Squash Agrodolce

ON YOGURT WITH DUKKAH

SQUASH AGRODOLCE

One 2 lb creamy-fleshed
    squash such as buttercup,
    seeded, peeled, and cut
    into medium chunks

½ cup apple cider vinegar

2 Tbsp extra-virgin olive oil,
    plus more for serving

1 Tbsp honey

½ red Thai chili, thinly sliced

½ tsp salt

DUKKAH

1 Tbsp whole coriander
    seeds

1 tsp whole red or black
    peppercorns

½ cup pine nuts or
    sunflower seeds or
    blanched hazelnuts

¼ cup sesame seeds

½ tsp salt

¼ tsp ground cardamom

BOWLS

2 cups plain whole-milk
    Greek yogurt or labneh
    (page 72) or cottage
    cheese

1 English cucumber,
    unpeeled and diced

Fresh cilantro or mint, for
    garnish

Lemon juice, for serving

Savory yogurt is a really unique brunch and lunch option, one that can be dressed up or down throughout the year depending on the season, your mood, and what's on hand. This version uses the flavors of agrodolce, an Italian sweet-and-sour sauce that creates a sticky, addictive coating on anything it's tossed with—here, it's tender, oven-baked squash. Dukkah, an Egyptian condiment, adds crunch and spice (not heat), while cucumber and lemon freshen things up. And I like to have a warm toasted sesame (always Montreal-style) bagel to scoop everything up with, although toasted naan, pita, flatbread, or sourdough toast would be awesome, too.

SERVES 4   ⏳ 50 MINUTES   🕐 5 DAYS FOR AGRODOLCE;
3 MONTHS FOR DUKKAH

1   For the squash agrodolce, preheat the oven to 375°F. In a 9- × 13-inch glass or ceramic baking dish, toss the squash with the vinegar, oil, honey, chili, and salt. Roast for 35 to 40 minutes, stirring halfway through, until tender and the liquid is sticky. Set aside.

2   For the dukkah, using a mortar and pestle or food processor, crush or pulse the coriander and peppercorns until finely ground. Add the remaining dukkah ingredients and crush or pulse to a medium-fine grind.

3   Add the dukkah mixture to a dry skillet and toast over medium heat, stirring almost constantly, for 4 to 6 minutes, until fragrant and medium-brown in color. Use it immediately or cool and store it in an airtight container in the refrigerator for up to 3 months.

4   If you are eating immediately, add the yogurt, labneh, or cottage cheese to serving bowls and drizzle with additional olive oil. Top the bowls with squash, cucumber, a generous sprinkle of dukkah,

a scattering of cilantro or mint, and a squeeze of lemon. If you are taking this to go, in each container or jar, add a layer of yogurt, a drizzle of additional olive oil, a handful of squash and cucumber, a generous sprinkle of dukkah, a scattering of cilantro or mint, and a squeeze of lemon. Seal everything up and refrigerate it until you are ready to take it with you. If you are taking this to work, keep your meal cold in the work refrigerator or in your lunch bag with a cooler pack.

Honey Bacon and
White Bean Mash Toast

(page 176)

The morning-after brunch is essential, and Geoff swears by bacon as a cure-all when you're feeling a little rough around the edges. Here, the remedy is presented as a fortifying, honey-shellacked treat with Italian-style white beans and super-crisp toast. Ideal with endless cups of pour-over coffee (page 176), slices of juicy grapefruit, and reminiscences about the night before.

SERVES 4   ⏳ 20 MINUTES   🕓 4 DAYS FOR WHITE BEAN MASH

1   For the honey bacon and toast, position a rack in the center of the oven. Preheat the oven to 400°F. Line a large rimmed baking sheet with parchment paper, add the bacon, and bake for 10 minutes. Transfer the bacon to a plate. Save some fat for brushing the toast and drain the remaining fat from the parchment and baking sheet; wipe the parchment with a paper towel. Return the bacon to the parchment and drizzle it evenly with the honey. Add the toast to the baking sheet beside the bacon and brush the toast with a bit of the reserved rendered bacon fat. Bake for 8 to 10 minutes longer, until the bacon is sticky and crisp, and the bread is toasted (extra-toasted is good here, as it won't become soggy as quickly). Meanwhile, prepare the beans.

2   For the beans, to a medium saucepan, add the beans, wine, oil, garlic, bay leaf, sage, and salt and pepper to taste. Bring to a boil, reduce to a simmer, cover, and cook for 8 to 10 minutes, until thickened. Mash some of the beans lightly with a fork to help thicken the sauce further, leaving plenty of texture.

3   To serve, add the toast to plates and top with the beans and bacon.

★ **RESTYLE: MAKE IT VEGGIE**
For a vegetarian version, or to simply switch it up, replace the honey bacon with a poached egg sprinkled with hot smoked paprika and a pinch of flaky salt. For a vegan version, leave off the topping altogether or bake up slices of smoked tofu brushed with maple syrup.

HONEY BACON AND TOAST

4 strips thick-cut bacon

1 Tbsp honey

4 slices sourdough or rustic bread of choice, thickly sliced

WHITE BEAN MASH

One 19 oz can white beans, drained and rinsed

½ cup white wine

2 Tbsp extra-virgin olive oil

1 clove garlic, smashed, kept whole

1 bay leaf

4 fresh sage leaves, shredded

Salt

Ground black pepper

Sweet Potato, Chard, and Smoked Cheddar Frittata

Serve this as part of a weekend spread, or pack up a wedge on the run. With no crust to get soggy, this frittata can be stored for a few days without compromising texture, taste, or appearance. Further adding to its flexibility, it can be served warm from the oven, at room temperature, or chilled.

SERVES 4 ⧗ 40 MINUTES ⏱ 3 DAYS

1 For the frittata, preheat the oven to 375°F. Line a 9-inch glass or ceramic pie plate with parchment paper, leaving overhang.

2 In a large high-sided skillet, heat the butter over medium-high heat until foamy. Sauté the sweet potato and onion for 12 to 15 minutes, until the sweet potatoes are mostly tender and beginning to brown. Stir in the chard stems and leaves and sauté until the greens are wilted and dark green, about 2 minutes. Smooth the mixture into the prepared pie plate.

3 In a large bowl, whisk the eggs with the milk, oregano, mustard, salt, nutmeg, and pepper to taste. Slowly pour the eggs over the vegetables. Top with the grated cheese.

4 Bake for 15 to 20 minutes, until puffed, dry on top, and cooked through. Check for doneness by inserting a paring knife into the center and testing on your finger for temperature—it should be really hot! If you want a golden brown top, broil on high for 2 to 3 minutes, until the cheese begins to brown. Cool for a few minutes and transfer to a cutting board using the overhanging parchment.

5 If you are eating immediately, slice the frittata into wedges and add to plates. In a large bowl, toss the mixed spring greens with vinaigrette to taste, then add them to the side of each plate and serve. If you are taking this to go, pack a slice of frittata and a handful of undressed greens in a container. Pack the dressing on the side in a separate small container or glass jar. Seal everything and refrigerate it until you are ready to take it with you. If you are not eating for a while, keep the frittata and greens in the work refrigerator or with a cooler pack in your lunch bag. Dress the greens before serving, and enjoy chilled or at room temperature.

2 Tbsp unsalted butter

1 large sweet potato, peeled and cut into small cubes

1 onion, diced

1 bunch Swiss chard, stems diced, leaves coarsely chopped

8 large eggs

⅓ cup milk of choice

½ tsp dry oregano

½ tsp dried mustard

½ tsp salt

¼ tsp grated nutmeg

Ground black pepper

½ cup grated smoked cheddar

6–8 cups mixed spring greens, for serving

Balsamic Vinaigrette (page 236)

Thanks to the sturdy, bold flavors of this frittata, it can
be served hot out of the oven, warm, at room temperature,
or chilled—a dream come true for entertaining and for
packed lunches. A simple side salad brightens up the plate,
but if tomatoes are in season, thick salted slices are my side
of choice.

Kombucha Americano

Half yogi, half hipster, this spritz uses kombucha, an effervescent probiotic tea, to liven up Americano cocktail-inspired add-ins for a brunchtime drink that looks like the sunrise—in case you happened to miss it.

For ease of serving, line up a few glasses and build all the drinks assembly line–style at the same time. For a non-alcoholic version, see the Lunch Note.

SERVES 1

1 Building in a glass on ice, add the Campari, vermouth, lemon juice, and kombucha. Top with a splash of soda water and garnish with the lemon wheel. Serve.

★ NON-ALCOHOLIC KOMBUCHA AMERICANO
Replace the Campari and vermouth with 2 ounces of grapefruit juice and ½ ounce of maple syrup or simple syrup (1:1 sugar to water, heated until dissolved). Garnish with a grapefruit wheel instead of a lemon wheel.

Ice

1 oz Campari

1 oz sweet vermouth

½ oz lemon juice

4 oz original or ginger kombucha

Soda water

Thinly sliced lemon wheel

Pour-Over Coffee

Brunch and a show. The pour-over method for preparing coffee is my preferred way to brew, offering a complex and elegant cup. It's a 5-minute ritual I look forward to every day, even more so when making brunch on the weekend. It does take some tools, though. A small digital kitchen scale is essential here, likewise a pour-over cone, filters, and a decanter. Investing in a burr grinder will make the best cup of coffee for any brew method, but is optional, and the gooseneck kettle for pour-over brewing is also optional. For a timer, I use the stopwatch on my phone to count up.

Many thanks to my partner, Geoff, who has worked in specialty coffee for the majority of his career, for his assistance with this recipe.

SERVES 2   ⧗ 5 MINUTES

RECOMMENDED EQUIPMENT

See the Gear Guide for full details (page 245).

Burr grinder

Gooseneck kettle

Pour-over cone

Decanter

Filters, as per your cone brand's requirements

Scale

Timer (I use my phone)

INGREDIENTS

500 g filtered water

30 g whole coffee beans

TIPS

· Start with well-roasted, well-sourced coffee. For a more floral, delicate-tasting cup, I like African coffees, especially in the summertime. When I want something heartier and more chocolaty, Colombian coffees are what I reach for. Specialty coffee roasters will give you the ability to choose your coffee's origin, and they'll supply tasting notes. And don't be afraid to ask your barista questions!

· Grinding fresh will make a remarkable difference in flavor, especially with a burr grinder, which makes sure all the pieces are the same size and can adjust the coarseness depending on what type of brew you're doing (pour-over, French press, etc.).

· It can take several brews to understand the timing of a pour-over, which takes about 3 minutes. But practicing this is fun, and even "mistakes" can be tasty. Pour in a slow, circular motion. This is where a gooseneck kettle is really handy—regular kettles can easily splash and burn you. After the initial pour, focus on pouring the water in a gentle, circular motion, focusing a few times on the center, with an ever-so-slightly more forceful pour.

SEE STEP-BY-STEP PHOTOS ON PAGES 178-179

1   Set the water on to boil in your kettle.

2   Weigh out the coffee and grind it to a medium-coarse texture, about the size of kosher salt.

3   Add the filter to the cone, folding the seam back if required (necessary in most Hario v60 pour-over models).

4   Rinse the filter with tap water (skip this step for pour-over filters with a wavy edge).

5   Place the cone with the filter over a decanter and add the ground coffee.

6   Place the decanter and cone with the filter and ground coffee on the scale, set to measure in grams, and tare (set to 0 grams). By this point, your water will likely be boiling. Time to brew!

7   Your pour-over should take about 3 minutes, give or take 30 seconds. Begin your timer and slowly pour over 100 grams of your just-boiled water, making sure to wet all the coffee (this is the "bloom"). Rest for 20 seconds.

8   Slowly pour over 200 grams more water in circles, waiting about 20 seconds to let most of the liquid filter through before adding the final amount of water.

9   Slowly pour over the final 200 grams of water in circles and let that filter through, stirring 3 times with a spoon during this process. This traps the finest particles at the top of filter, allowing the rest to filter through in the correct time. Your 3 minutes, give or take 30 seconds, should be up now.

10 Compost your filter containing the grounds, stir the coffee with a clean spoon or give it a swirl, and pour it into warmed mugs. Enjoy.

1-5

6

8

7

POUR-OVER COFFEE

Images correspond to
steps on page 177

9

10

CHAPTER 8

Picnic Baskets

IN THE SUMMER, I live for picnics. They are pure pleasure. They can be potluck-style, where you pick a meeting place and call your friends to bring a dish, or intimate affairs with someone special.

I like to plan and pack a simple themed menu that can suit any adventure, from classic blanketed picnics in the park to on-the-move road trip meals and beyond. But if the baskets I've put together here don't do it for you, or if you're looking to add or subtract one meal for another, any *Modern Lunch* recipe that's packable and doesn't require reheating (unless you've got the power of a campfire or camp stove) is suitable for your midday movable feast.

English Picnic

Shopping at an outdoor market and preparing a spread based on what I find is my favorite way to eat midday, especially on a weekend. With a menu in mind, I'm less likely to overdo it, but I do encourage you to swap in with what's fresh, local, and appealing in your area, where appropriate. This picnic is inspired by my time living in London, England, where one is spoiled for choice when it comes to weekend market options.

SERVES 4

MENU

Potted Mackerel (page 185)

Seasonal vegetables

Cheese

Bread

Whole-Wheat Strawberry Shortcake Scones with Cardamom Cream (page 186)

Beer or wine

Potted Mackerel

SERVES 4　⏳ 10 MINUTES　🕐 2 WEEKS

1　Add the mackerel to a large bowl and finely flake using your fingers, discarding any stray pin bones.

2　Switch to a spoon and mix in the lemon zest, lemon juice, dill, chili, nutmeg, and cloves. Set aside.

3　In a small saucepan, melt the butter until just liquefied. Measure out 3 tablespoons of melted butter and add to the mackerel mixture, mixing well to combine.

4　Press the mackerel mixture into two small shallow glass jars or ramekins, taking care to gently but firmly secure the mixture without air pockets; smooth the tops. Clean the sides of the jars and divide the remaining butter over top of the pressed mackerel mixture. Before the butter sets, add a few fronds of dill. Chill for at least 2 hours, until the butter is firm. Cover and continue to store in the refrigerator until you are ready to use it, up to 2 weeks.

5　Serve with a spritz of lemon, spread onto baguette, crostini, crackers, or endive.

5 oz (½ whole) smoked mackerel, skin and bones removed (DIY or ask the fishmonger)

1 tsp lemon zest

2 Tbsp lemon juice

1 tsp chopped fresh dill, plus more for garnish

⅛ tsp minced fresh red Thai chili

Good pinch of grated nutmeg

Good pinch of ground cloves

½ cup unsalted butter

Lemon wedges, for serving

Whole-Wheat Strawberry Shortcake Scones

WITH CARDAMOM CREAM

SERVES 6 ⧖ 20 MINUTES ⏱ 1 DAY FOR SCONES AND
CARDAMOM CREAM; 2 DAYS FOR STRAWBERRIES

SCONES

2 cups whole-wheat flour,
plus more for rolling

2 Tbsp wheat germ or
quick-cooking rolled oats

3 Tbsp turbinado sugar,
divided

1 Tbsp baking powder

½ tsp salt

2 Tbsp cold unsalted butter,
cubed

¼ cup coconut oil, solid,
room temperature

¾ cup buttermilk, plus
more for brushing

½ tsp citrus zest
(grapefruit, lemon,
orange, or lime)

STRAWBERRIES

4 cups fresh strawberries,
hulled and sliced

2 Tbsp turbinado sugar

1 tsp citrus juice (grapefruit,
lemon, orange, or lime)

½ tsp vanilla extract

CARDAMOM CREAM

2 cups whipping cream

2 Tbsp buttermilk or sour
cream

1 Tbsp turbinado sugar

¼ tsp ground cardamom

1   For the biscuits, preheat the oven to 450°F.

2   In a large bowl, mix the flour, wheat germ or oats, 2 tablespoons of sugar, baking powder, and salt until fully combined. Using a pastry cutter or quickly with forks or your fingers, cut in the butter and coconut oil until only pea-sized pieces remain and the mixture is sandy in texture. Stir in the buttermilk and citrus zest, and mix briefly until the mixture is combined and dough retains its shape when formed into a ball.

3   Form the mixture into a 1- to 2-inch-high disk on parchment paper using lightly floured hands or a rolling pin. Using a biscuit cutter or drinking glass, cut round biscuits (about 3 to 4 inches in diameter) and space evenly on a large rimmed baking sheet. Re-form the scraps and cut into biscuits until dough is used up, for 6 biscuits.

4   Brush the tops of the biscuits with a bit of buttermilk and sprinkle with the remaining 1 tablespoon of sugar. Bake for 12 to 15 minutes, until the biscuits are springy when touched and golden brown. Let cool completely on the tray. Store loosely covered at room temperature up to 1 day or freeze for up to 3 months. If you are making these ahead, reheat in a 300°F oven for 5 to 10 minutes (fresh, or frozen and defrosted) to restore the top crust before serving.

5   For the strawberries, mix the strawberries, sugar, citrus juice, and vanilla together and set aside to macerate for 5 to 10 minutes, until the strawberries start to release their juices. Refrigerate in an airtight container for up to 2 days.

6   For the cardamom cream, whip the cream until soft to medium peaks form. Whisk in the buttermilk or sour cream, sugar, and cardamom. Refrigerate in an airtight container for up to 1 day.

7   To assemble, immediately before serving, slice the biscuits in half horizontally. Put a dollop of cream on the bottom biscuit half and cover with macerated strawberries. Top with the second biscuit half and serve.

PICNIC ASSEMBLY

1   Start with packing fridge-cold potted mackerel, cheese, strawberries, cream, and beverages.

2   Lay everything out on a large table or blanket. Pour beverages. Spread mackerel and/or cheese onto bread, garnish with vegetables, and season with a squeeze of lemon.

3   Finish your picnic with strawberry shortcake scones (assembly directions in recipe).

Camping

On my first backcountry camping trip, we hiked for
5 hours—in and out—on one of the toughest sections
of the Bruce Trail, in Ontario, carrying 70-pound
backpacks. There were tears, bruises, mini fits, and a
surprise mountain scaling adventure to tackle. It
ended by us getting a ride out of the opposite trail
entrance in the back of a pickup truck, followed by our
first successful highway hitchhiking endeavor, made
possible thanks to a kind soul who drove us all the way
back to our car. I have never been so spent, and proud,
in my life. After living off packaged and dried foods,
spoonfuls of peanut butter, and cans of tuna for 2 days,
I dreamt of a more glamorous camping menu, and
these recipes were the result. They would suit "glamp-
ing," car camping, and day hikes with a mini stove, but
would do well in the backyard, too.

SERVES 4

MENU

Just-Add-Water Miso, Sweet Potato, and Soba Ramen
(page 45)

Honey Marshmallow S'mores (page 191)

Mulled Spiked Cider (page 193)

Honey Marshmallow S'mores

Step 1: Honey Marshmallows

MAKES 24 REGULAR MARSHMALLOWS OR 12 EXTRA-LARGE MARSHMALLOWS ⧗ 13 HOURS ⊙ 1 MONTH

1 Lightly grease an 8- × 8-inch square baking pan with oil. Line with parchment paper so all sides are covered, leaving some to overhang the edges.

2 In a medium bowl, combine the icing sugar and cornstarch. Lightly grease the parchment and dust with the icing sugar mixture to cover the bottom and sides. Tap out the excess sugar and set aside. Do not discard.

3 Add ⅓ cup of water to the bowl of a stand mixer fitted with a whisk attachment. Sprinkle in gelatin and let bloom at least 10 minutes.

4 In a medium saucepan, add the remaining ⅓ cup water, the demerara sugar, honey, and cane sugar. Heat over medium-high heat until the sugar is dissolved and a candy thermometer registers 240°F, 4 to 6 minutes.

5 Turn the stand mixer on low and carefully drizzle the melted sugar mixture into gelatin mixture. Turn the speed to medium for 1 minute, and then to high for 10 minutes, or until mixture is pale brown and very fluffy. Quickly beat in the vanilla and salt.

6 Transfer the marshmallow mixture to the prepared baking pan and smooth the top. Dust your hands generously with the icing sugar mixture, and press gently and evenly to level the marshmallow mixture. Let cool uncovered for at least 12 hours, until set.

7 Line a large baking sheet with parchment paper. To slice, remove the marshmallow from the parchment and coat a knife with the icing sugar mixture. Slice into 12 extra-large or 24 regular squares, cleaning and coating the knife as necessary. Toss with more icing sugar mixture, dust off the excess, and set on the prepared baking sheet. Set aside for 2 to 4 hours at room temperature.

8 Wrap each marshmallow in parchment. Store in an airtight container for up to 1 month.

Neutral oil, for greasing

½ cup organic icing sugar, gluten-free if necessary

½ cup organic cornstarch, gluten-free if necessary

⅔ cup water, divided

½ oz (2 packages, about 4 tsp) gelatin

¾ cup demerara sugar

⅔ cup honey

¼ cup fine evaporated cane sugar

1 Tbsp vanilla extract

¼ tsp salt

Step 2: Graham Crackers

SMAKES 24 (FOR 12 S'MORES)   ⧖ 40 MINUTES   ⊙ 1 WEEK

2 cups light spelt flour or
  whole-wheat flour, plus
  more for rolling

⅓ cup finely chopped
  pecans (from ½ cup
  pecan halves)

2 Tbsp ground flaxseed

¼ tsp salt

½ cup coconut oil, melted

¼ cup plus 1 Tbsp water

2 Tbsp honey

1 Tbsp molasses

½ tsp vanilla extract

1   In a large bowl, combine the flour, pecans, flaxseed, and salt.

2   In a medium bowl, combine the coconut oil, water, honey, molasses, and vanilla. Stir the coconut oil mixture into the flour mixture until fully combined. Rest the dough for 10 minutes to allow the flour to absorb the liquid.

3   Preheat the oven to 350°F. Line a large rimmed baking sheet with parchment paper.

4   On a lightly floured surface or canvas rolling mat, roll the dough to ¼- to ⅛-inch thickness. Slice into 3- × 3-inch squares. Keep rerolling and cutting the remaining dough. Line the squares up beside each other (they can be very close as they don't spread, but make sure they aren't touching) and prick a few times with a fork. Bake for 15 to 20 minutes, until deep brown and crisp. Cool completely on the baking sheet. Store in an airtight container at room temperature for up to 1 week or freeze for up to 2 months.

Step 3: S'mores

SERVES 12

Two 3½ oz bars dark
  chocolate, broken into
  2-inch squares

24 Graham Crackers

12 small Honey
  Marshmallows

Long twigs, for toasting

1   Place chocolate squares on half the graham crackers (1 square on each).

2   Skewer the marshmallows on twigs (use 2 or 3 twigs side by side for an extra-large marshmallow, otherwise it will fall off!) and toast over your fire (or, if you're at home, toast briefly under the broiler, over a tea light, or with a kitchen blowtorch).

3   Place each toasted marshmallow on top of chocolate-topped graham cracker and sandwich with a plain graham cracker. Enjoy (and how could you not?).

Mulled Spiked Cider

SERVES 4   ⧗ 1 HOUR   ⟳ 3 DAYS

4 cups apple cider (non-alcoholic)

2 thick strips orange peel, plus more for serving

1 cinnamon stick, plus more for serving

2 whole cloves

Whole star anise

Whiskey, to taste

1   In a large fireproof or regular pot or slow cooker, heat the cider, orange peel, cinnamon, cloves, and star anise, covered, over low heat for 1 to 4 hours, until the spices are infused into the cider and the mixture is hot. Spike each mug with whiskey to taste, and ladle in the hot cider. Serve garnished with a fresh cinnamon stick for stirring and a fresh orange peel.

PICNIC ASSEMBLY

1   When packing, start with fridge-cold ramen jars and cider. Pack the s'more components (marshmallows, crackers, and chocolate) outside the cooler.

2   Prepare the cider according to recipe directions (above).

3   Boil water for the ramen in a fireproof pot or on a camp stove, and prepare according to recipe directions (page 45).

4   To finish the picnic, prepare s'mores according to recipe directions (above). If you have lit a fire, be sure to extinguish it!

Waterfront

Growing up, my siblings and I were lucky to spend Northern Ontario summers at our family cottage. Each day after breakfast, we would take snacks and drinks down the hill to the dock, swimming and fishing and boating and grazing all afternoon, until the sun was setting and we could smell dinner up the hill. The roads leading to our cottage were lined with wild raspberry bushes. We would pick the berries and adorn our morning cereal and evening vanilla ice cream with them.

As an adult, I still gravitate toward the gentle din of the water during the summertime, packing lunches, snacks, and even weeknight after-work dinners to be enjoyed by the bay. This is my grown-up version of the food we would snack on at our family cottage.

SERVES 4

MENU

Farro, Beet, Asparagus, and Watercress Picnic Salad (page 128)

Cold Noodle Salad with Smoked Tofu and Miso-Sesame Dressing (page 25)

Watermelon slices

Grapefruit and Mint Palomas (page 196)

Grapefruit and Mint Palomas

Handful fresh mint leaves

Ice

Two 12 oz cans or one 25 oz
bottle Italian grapefruit
soda, such as San
Pellegrino

½–1 cup mescal or tequila,
to your preference

¼ cup lime juice

One 12 oz can club soda
(optional)

Salt, to taste

SERVES 4   ⏳ 5 MINUTES

1   Smack the mint leaves between your hands to release the
oils and add to 4 tall glasses along with the ice. Top each glass
with ½ can (¾ cup) of grapefruit soda, 2 Tbsp (1 ounce) to ¼ cup
(2 ounces) of mescal or tequila (less for a weaker drink and more
for a stronger drink), and 1 tablespoon (½ ounce) of lime juice.
Top with a splash of club soda (if using) and a pinch of salt. Serve.

PICNIC ASSEMBLY

1   Before you begin packing, make sure everything is fridge-cold.

2   Lay everything out on a large table or blanket, make the palomas,
and enjoy.

Road Trip

A few years ago, Geoff and I drove down the Pacific Coast Highway, stopping along the way to take photos, drink coffee, soak in the best sunset in the world, and, of course, eat. Since then, we've had many road trips together, and when it comes to the food, we turn to brighter, fresher tastes to keep our spirits and energy levels high. This menu here delivers those crucial road trip elements, with an electric wake-up call supplied by hydrating turmeric tonics.

SERVES 4

MENU

Cauliflower Fatteh with Pine Nuts and Dates (page 40)

Root vegetable chips (store-bought)

Berry and Apple Oat Squares (page 216)

Sparkling Turmeric, Ginger, and Lemon Tonic (page 200)

Sparkling Turmeric, Ginger, and Lemon Tonic

SERVES 4 ⏳ 10 MINUTES ⏱ 1 MONTH (WITHOUT ICE OR CLUB SODA)

Zest of 1 lemon

⅓ cup fresh lemon juice

¼ cup packed coarsely chopped fresh, organic ginger (peeled if not organic)

¼ cup raw honey

2 Tbsp ground turmeric

Pinch of salt

Pinch of ground black pepper

Ice, as needed

Two 12 oz cans club soda

1 Add all the tonic ingredients except ice and club soda to a blender and puree until smooth.

2 Using a fine-mesh sieve lined with a double layer of cheesecloth, strain into a clean jar, pressing or squeezing to extract the ginger juice. Discard the pulp or save it to mix into curries or soups— kind of like a homemade curry paste. Refrigerate the strained juice in an airtight container for up to 1 month.

3 When you're ready to serve, add the ice to glasses, followed by 1 to 2 tablespoons of the turmeric mixture per glass, to taste. Top with club soda and serve.

PICNIC ASSEMBLY

1 When you begin packing, make sure that all the ingredients are fridge-cold.

2 Once you've found the perfect picnic spot, prepare the turmeric tonics, take out your jars, open the chips, and enjoy.

PART IV

MAKE LUNCH SPECIAL

(on lunch clubs and simple snacks)

I KNOW IT'S A BIG ASK to have you prepare lunches for the week and maybe the weekend, *and* think about snacks and, now, lunch clubs, but this is the chapter for those who are looking for something more than just the food. This is where the Modern Lunch Club (MLC) comes in. I'll start with that.

The MLC is about sharing a meal, communing around a table to see other styles of cooking, new flavors, and fresh presentations, and to hear the stories attached to the recipes (or some hot gossip). As someone who has had many lunch meetings at restaurants, I've found that an MLC-style lunch, even when business has to be discussed, is far more effective and productive. Sharing homemade food (in real life, not online), whether made by you or someone else, allows everyone to relax and "turn off" for a bit. Having a lunch club in your life, even if meetings are rare, is incredibly rewarding.

Okay, I realize I just said this section is about "more than just the food," but really, when you need a snack, it's about the food. At this point in my personal lunch game, snacks are an integral part of my weekly midday meal prep. A snack can be as simple as hummus and carrot sticks, sliced apple with peanut butter, or a constructed-on-the-fly jar of yogurt and granola (I believe common breakfast items make fantastic afternoon snacks). Or dirty a few more dishes and whip up an energy bar, fruit and oat square, or healthy and nostalgic chocolate pudding cup—they're all here in this chapter, and snacks have no rules.

If you're in search of a no-fuss sweet for your Modern Lunch Club meeting, workplace treat (my, what lucky coworkers you have!), afternoon meeting, or midday weekend entertaining, you'll find a few more wholesome (but so, so good) options here that fit the bill.

This part of the book is optional, but recommended, if not for now, then for a few months from now, when you're in the swing of preparing a homemade lunch on the regular.

Modern Lunch Club

NOW THAT YOU'RE in the habit of packing a lunch, it's time to share the joys with colleagues, friends, and family, with your very own Modern Lunch Club.

A Modern Lunch Club involves a solid, reliable group of food lovers who contribute one "family" meal per week or month. Each member takes their turn on the rotation, bringing a complete recipe or several potluck-style recipes to share. To make this happen, you'll need at least 2 people to participate, preferably 4 to 6. It's about inclusivity, but if you have too many people, there gets to be too much food for one person to carry (especially on public transit).

You can call it whatever you like, but the premise of the Modern Lunch Club remains the same: it's a way to connect, reflect, and share a meal with others when time allows, instead of eating on the go, eating at your desk, or (gasp) skipping lunch.

How It Works

There's more than one way to build your lunch club.

OPTION 1: ONE MEMBER PER CYCLE

1 Pick one day each week or one day each month when the lunch club will meet.

2 Have each member sign up for a date.

3 On each member's date, that member brings lunch for the entire group.

OPTION 2: POTLUCK EVERY CYCLE

1 Pick one day each week or one day each month when the lunch club will meet.

2 If you don't want to risk a true potluck—meaning what shows up on the table from other guests is a surprise to all—make a sign-up sheet so you know you'll have a balanced lunchtime meal. You don't necessarily want to end up with 5 kale salads, for example.

3 Have everyone bring a meal to share, potluck-style.

OPTION 3: THEMED (VIA OPTION 1 OR OPTION 2)

1 Pick one day each week or one day each month when the lunch club will meet.

2 Pick a theme for the lunch club in general, or for each turn. This could be a salad-only club, a cook the world club, a soup club, etc.

3 Have each member sign up for their date (see Option 1) or embrace potluck-style club meetings (see Option 2).

4 On each member's date, that member brings the themed lunch for the entire group (see Option 1), or have everyone bring a part of the themed meal to share potluck-style (see Option 2).

Your lunch club will take a small amount of organizing, but the benefits outweigh the costs.

Here's What You Get from Setting Up a Lunch Club

· A (sometimes free) homemade lunch 1 to 4 times per month.

· A chance to experience a new cuisine, recipe, or style of cooking you may not know about, or that you may be shy about trying yourself.

· Bonding time with your lunch club buddies and the chance to meet new friends.

· An opportunity to impress your boss, colleagues, employees, friends, or family by bringing the team together.

Lunch Club Success Tips

MAKE IT A MONDAY   The lunch club is more likely to succeed when the person or people cooking have more time to cook. Preparing the meal for Monday on Sunday avoids the busy trap Monday-to-Friday meal prep faces (but see next tip). Also, this means you'll have something at the beginning of the week to look forward to.

BE CONSISTENT   This is key. Be sure to meet on the same day and at the same time each week or month for best results. If you work from home, are a stay-at-home parent, or just find yourself not wanting to mix work with pleasure, your lunch club can meet any day that works best. This could be Sunday afternoon or Wednesday at 1 p.m., if that's what works for you.

WORKPLACE ESSENTIALS   Does your work have a refrigerator? Hot plate? Toaster? Toaster oven? Take all of these things into consideration when forming the menu. If you're hosting your lunch club at home, this likely isn't an issue, so for work menus, meals that can be enjoyed at room temperature or cold are best.

DIETARY RESTRICTIONS   Take note of all member allergies or dietary restrictions. If several come up, think of this as a way to explore a new way of cooking as opposed to navigating an annoying roadblock. If it's as simple as vegetarians versus meat eaters, meals that can be adapted, like DIY tacos or lettuce wraps with various proteins (beans, tofu, chicken, salmon), mean everyone can take part.

SET A BUDGET   The lunch club shouldn't break the bank. A budget of $20 to $50 should be more than enough if you keep to the recommended 4 to 6 people.

BRING YOUR OWN VS. GROUP LUNCHWARE POOL
One option is to have each member responsible for their own plate, bowl, utensils, etc. (at work or at a picnic). Another option is to invest as a group in inexpensive lunchware. Plastic is okay, but it's not very pleasant to eat from. A set of varied IKEA dishes for 4 people can cost as low as $25, and split among the club members, this becomes very affordable. Secondhand stores carry dishes and utensils, too. Or your workplace may already have what you need.

KEEP IT SIMPLE   The goal is not to dread your turn to cook. Share something simple that you're excited about. Cooked brown rice, kale salad, hard-boiled eggs, and seasonal fruit for dessert is not only delicious but healthy and quick to prepare the night before, and keeps well overnight. One-pot meals served with sourdough bread or a simple salad are another stellar lunch club choice.

MIX IT UP   Huddle in the lunchroom. Go to your work's common room. In the nice weather, go outside for a picnic. Find a park. Congregate around a member's desk. If you are hosting a lunch club at home, hop to a different member's house each time (probably the one cooking that cycle) or meet at the beach. Have a dynamic Modern Lunch Club HQ and be forever inspired.

PLAN B   Something, someday, will happen. Maybe the member who is to cook for the group will wake up with the flu. Maybe you'll have a meeting that runs into your club time. Stuff happens. Don't feel bad about going out to lunch that day if it does. Reschedule the lunch club for the following day, or another day that works.

Modern Lunch Club Menus

Making the menu is the fun part! Try one of the themes I've noted below, or create your own using any of the packable recipes from the book.

DOUBLE THE FOLLOWING RECIPES AS NEEDED

Middle Eastern Menu

- Sheet-Pan Persian Lemon Chicken (page 107)
- Lemony Barley and Roasted Carrot Salad with Goat Cheese (page 138)
- Whole Grapefruit and Almond Cake (page 221)

Healthy Comfort Food Menu

- Savory Vegetable Cobbler (page 53)
- Sunday Kale Salad (page 131)
- Berry and Apple Oat Squares (page 216)

Warming Curry Menu

- Pantry Dal with Raita, Brown Rice, and Mango (page 81)
- fresh pineapple with lime and chili

West Coast Inspired Menu

- California Lunch Bowl (page 95)
- Chicken, Eggplant, and Basil Wraps with Cashews (page 86)
- Sparkling Turmeric, Ginger, and Lemon Tonic (page 200)
- Cashew, Coconut, and Banana Bars (page 218)

Build Your Own Lunch Bowl Menu

· baby arugula (1 to 2 clamshell packs)

· Balsamic Vinaigrette (page 236)

· Roasted Vegetables (page 242)

· Hummus (page 147)

· Grilled chicken (page 239) or hard-boiled eggs (page 238)

· Quinoa (page 242)

Many Salads Menu

· Butternut Squash Kale Salad with Roasted Garlic Dressing (page 124)

· Farro, Beet, Asparagus, and Watercress Picnic Salad (page 128)

· Chicken, Celery, and Apple Waldorf with Oat Groats (page 31)

· sliced watermelon

Meatless Menu

· Brussels Sprout, Grape, and Goat Cheese Pizza (page 109)

· French Lentil Salad with Roasted Radishes, Peas, and Eggs (page 39)

· dark chocolate and roasted almonds

Brunch for Lunch Menu

· Sweet Potato, Chard, and Smoked Cheddar Frittata (page 172)

· 9-Layer Salad with Lemon Curry Dressing (page 20)

· strained Yogurt (page 72) with seasonal fruit

Communal Platter Menu

· A Gathered Platter (page 145)

· Fresh strawberries to dip in Express Chocolate Pudding Cups (page 215)

CHAPTER 10

Lunchbox Treasures

NOT ESSENTIAL TO WINNING the lunch game but quite special to find in your bag or stashed away in your home freezer, snacks and healthy-ish sweets are key to a happy day. From no-recipe ideas that are as simple as can be to nostalgic cups of instant chocolate pudding made with a surprise ingredient, to frozen treats that you can magically pop out of the freezer when entertaining on a summer weekend, there's a pleasure-enhancing, hunger-subduing solution here for any time of the day.

Express Chocolate Pudding Cups

This tastes nearly identical to the real thing, but is far healthier, packed with protein, and lower in sugar. The only bad thing about this recipe is that there's no pudding-cup top to peel off and lick. Fruit and cream are optional but definitely add something special.

SERVES 4   ⧗ 10 MINUTES   ⏱ 1 WEEK

1   For the pudding, in a food processor or blender, blend the tofu until it is smooth, with no visible lumps. Add the cocoa powder, honey or maple syrup, vanilla, and salt and puree until completely smooth and creamy. Blend in the coconut oil until just combined, being sure not to over-blend or the mixture will turn gritty. If it's so thick the machine isn't moving, blend in a splash of milk (but be sure to not exceed ¼ cup).

2   To serve, spoon the blended chocolate mixture into a container or large jar to store, or individual containers or jars to take to work. Seal and refrigerate until chilled and set, about 1 hour and up to 1 week. The liquid may separate, which is normal, so give it a quick stir before serving. Once the pudding is chilled and set, top it with berries and cream, if desired. If taking it to work, keep the pudding refrigerated until you are ready to eat it.

★ CHOCOLATE + . . .
Chocolate pudding can be enhanced finely ground or instant coffee grounds (1 teaspoon), ground cinnamon (¼ teaspoon), orange zest (¼ teaspoon), orange flower water (¼ teaspoon), mint oil (¹⁄₁₆ teaspoon), cayenne (pinch), flaky sea salt (pinch), or peanut butter (2 tablespoons). You can always add, but you can't take away, so use a light hand to start.

One 16 oz package medium-firm tofu, drained (medium-firm is important; do not use extra-firm)

¼ cup unsweetened cocoa powder

¼ cup honey or maple syrup

½ tsp vanilla extract

¼ tsp salt

3 Tbsp coconut oil, melted

Milk of choice, if needed

Diced fresh strawberries or raspberries, for serving (optional)

Whipped cream, for serving (optional)

Berry and Apple Oat Squares

This recipe, with a gluten-free, flour-free oat crust bound with buttery coconut oil, maple syrup, and cinnamon, holds a naturally sweet fruit filling of apples and berries. A milky cappuccino or hot cup of tea pairs particularly well with these squares for a little mid-afternoon boost.

MAKES 12   ⏳ 1 HOUR   🕐 4 DAYS

FILLING

3 apples, peeled and
   coarsely chopped

1 cup fresh or frozen
   raspberries

½ cup water

½ tsp cinnamon

½ tsp vanilla extract

CRUST

4 cups quick-cooking rolled
   oats, divided, or 3 cups oat
   flour + 1 cup rolled oats

½ tsp ground cinnamon

½ tsp salt

½ cup coconut oil, melted

½ cup maple syrup

★ **FRUIT FILLING
SWITCH-UP**

Think seasonally and locally. Replace the apples and raspberries with blueberries and peaches, blackberries and plums, etc. Fresh or frozen fruits both work, allowing you to take this bar for lunch year-round.

1   For the filling, in a medium saucepan, combine the apples, raspberries, water, and cinnamon. Bring to a boil, reduce to a simmer, and cook for 10 minutes, until the fruit is very tender and jam-like in consistency. Transfer to a blender or food processor, add the vanilla, and blend until the mixture has the texture of applesauce. Set aside.

2   For the crust, preheat the oven to 350°F. Line an 8- × 8-inch baking pan with parchment paper.

3   Blend 3 cups of the oats in a blender or food processor until the grains have the texture of flour (or use 3 cups of prepared oat flour).

4   To a large bowl, transfer the blended oat flour along with the remaining 1 cup of whole oats, cinnamon, and salt; mix to combine. Mix in the coconut oil and maple syrup until fully incorporated.

5   To make the squares, firmly press two-thirds of the crust into the bottom of the prepared pan, spread the blended filling on top, and crumble over the remaining one-third of crust.

6   Bake for 40 to 45 minutes, until the top is dry and beginning to brown. Cool in the pan for 15 minutes, remove from the pan, and let cool completely on a wire rack for at least 2 hours before slicing. Once cool, slice into 12 squares and store in an airtight container at room temperature for up to 4 days, or freeze for up to 2 months. To pack, wrap the squares in parchment, plastic, foil, or beeswax wrap.

Power Snacks

These snacks have gone to coffee farms in rural Guatemala, backcountry trails in Northern Canada, and rugged mountains in Snowdonia, Wales. So I can say this with great certainty: these travel well (my partner calls these "Adventure Bites"). They're a nutritious work snack, and my favorite road snack, providing energy via protein, fiber, and nourishing fat. Once you're comfortable with the proportions, try making your own bar flavors.

Cashew, Coconut, and Banana Bars

MAKES 8 ⧖ 1 HOUR 10 MINUTES ⊕ 1 MONTH

35 tender dates, pitted

½ cup unsalted raw cashews

½ cup (1¼ oz) unsweetened shredded coconut

½ cup banana chips

2 Tbsp dark chocolate chips (optional)

Pinch of salt

1 Add the dates, cashews, coconut, banana chips, chocolate chips (if using), and salt to a food processor. Alternate between blending and pulsing for about 30 seconds to crush large pieces, until the mixture is sticky and holds together when squeezed.

2 Line a standard loaf pan with plastic wrap or parchment paper and press in the mixture as tightly as possible. Refrigerate for 1 hour, remove from the pan, and cut into 8 bars.

3 Wrap the bars in plastic wrap and store them in an airtight container at room temperature for up to 1 month.

Cranberry, Oatmeal, and Walnut Bites

MAKES 8 ⧖ 1 HOUR 10 MINUTES ⊕ 1 MONTH

25 tender dates, pitted

½ cup dried cranberries

1 cup unsalted raw or roasted walnuts

⅓ cup quick-cooking rolled oats

Pinch of grated nutmeg

Pinch of salt

1 Add the dates, cranberries, walnuts, oats, nutmeg, and salt to a food processor. Pulse the mixture on and off for 30 seconds to chop the larger pieces, until it's sticky and holds together when squeezed.

2 Roll the mixture into balls.

3 Wrap each bite in plastic wrap or layer the bites between parchment paper in an airtight container, and store at room temperature for up to 1 month.

Vanilla, Almond, and Cardamom Bars

MAKES 8 ⏳ 1 HOUR 10 MINUTES ⏱ 1 MONTH

1 Add the dates, almonds, vanilla, almond extract, cardamom, and salt to a food processor. Pulse the mixture for 30 seconds to break up the nuts, and continue to pulse until it holds together when squeezed.

2 Line a standard loaf pan with plastic wrap or parchment paper and press in the mixture as tightly as possible. Refrigerate for 1 hour, remove from the pan, and cut into 8 bars.

3 Wrap the bars in plastic wrap and store them in an airtight container at room temperature for up to 1 month.

35 tender dates, pitted

1¼ cups unsalted raw or roasted almonds

1 tsp vanilla extract

⅛ tsp almond extract

Pinch of ground cardamom

Pinch of salt

★ EVEN MORE POWER SNACK FORMULAS

· dates + hemp + dried mulberries + cacao nibs

· dates + sunflower seeds + cashews + almonds + pumpkin seeds

· dates + almonds + cocoa + dark chocolate chunks + dried cherries

Whole Grapefruit and Almond Cake

I have a penchant for any recipe with grapefruit. Its bitter, juicy interior wakes up everything it's added to—and this cake is no exception. Using just a food processor, an entire grapefruit (yes, both the skin and flesh), and a few other sweetening, aromatizing, and binding ingredients, a brunch, lunch, or teatime treat (preferably paired with a strong black or Earl Grey tea) can be yours. The inspiration for this recipe comes from Anneka Manning's whole orange cake, from her *BakeClass* cookbook, a book that has taught me the joys of simple baked goods done very, very well.

SERVES 8 TO 10   ⧗ 3 HOURS 30 MINUTES   ⏱ 4 DAYS

1 For the cake, preheat the oven to 325°F. Grease and flour an 8-inch springform or cake pan.

2 In a food processor, pulse the grapefruit until finely chopped. Add the granulated sugar, butter, eggs, and almond extract, and puree until blended. Add the flour, baking powder, baking soda, and salt to the grapefruit mixture, and puree briefly until just combined. Smooth the batter into the prepared pan and bake for 45 to 50 minutes, or until a toothpick inserted in the center comes out clean and the top is a lovely golden brown. Cool in the pan for 10 minutes before removing the cake to a wire cooling rack. Let cool completely, about 2 hours.

3 For the glaze, in a small bowl, combine the icing sugar, 5 teaspoons of the grapefruit juice or orange juice, and the almond extract. If needed, add more juice, 1 teaspoon at a time, until the mixture is runny enough to drizzle.

CONTINUED

WHOLE GRAPEFRUIT AND ALMOND CAKE

1 large red grapefruit, washed, quartered, and seeds removed

1 cup granulated sugar

½ cup unsalted butter, melted, plus more for pan

2 large eggs

¼ tsp almond extract

1½ cups plus 2 Tbsp unbleached all-purpose flour, plus more for pan

1¾ tsp baking powder

½ tsp baking soda

½ tsp salt

GRAPEFRUIT GLAZE

1 cup icing sugar

5–7 tsp grapefruit juice or orange juice, as needed

¼ tsp almond extract

¼ cup sliced almonds

4   To glaze the cake, place a large baking sheet or piece of parchment paper under the wire cooling rack to catch any drips. Spread the glaze over the cake, allowing it to drip down the sides. Before the glaze sets, evenly sprinkle on the sliced almonds. Allow the glaze to set until it is matte and dry on top, about 30 minutes, before slicing and serving. Store in an airtight container at room temperature for up to 4 days. To pack, wrap a slice of cake in parchment, plastic, foil, or beeswax wrap.

★ **RESTYLE: WHOLE ORANGE, ALMOND, AND OLIVE OIL CAKE**
If you want a cake with less bitter notes, use a big, juicy navel orange in place of the grapefruit. In this case, you can also replace the melted butter with a light-tasting olive oil for a slice reminiscent of classic olive oil orange cake.

Savory and Sweet No-Recipe Snack Solutions

Fresh ingredients and pantry staples you may already have on hand can make a range of fresh, truly satisfying snacks. And in a pinch, you can build an entire lunch "main" around snacks, so here I've outlined what that could look like for you, too.

Savory Snacks

- air-popped popcorn + flaky salt

- cheese + crackers + dates

- cherry tomatoes + bocconcini

- watermelon or cantaloupe + feta + black pepper

- chilled silken tofu + miso dressing + sliced green onions

- crudités + Greek yogurt dressed with chives

- half avocado + olive oil + flaky salt

- hard-boiled eggs

- hummus + crudités + flatbread

- leftover brown rice + tamari + toasted sesame oil + sesame seeds

- leftover cooked chicken + mustard + apple

- leftover roasted sweet potato + hummus

- yogurt + cucumber + tamari almonds + olive oil

Sweet Snacks

- apple + nut butter or aged cheddar

- banana + raw cashews

- clementine + energy bar

- dark chocolate + raw almonds

- leftover brown rice + maple syrup + roasted almonds

· nuts + dried fruit + coconut chips

· smoothie: banana + date + coconut milk + nutmeg

· smoothie: berry + Greek yogurt + honey

· toast + peanut butter + honey + flaky salt

· yogurt + walnuts + honey + sprinkle of cinnamon

· yogurt + frozen mango + lime juice + cashews + dark chocolate

· yogurt + granola

Last-Minute Mini Meals and Snack Lunches

When you're in a hurry, pull this and that from the refrigerator to make a snacky lunch in a snap that you can graze on all workday long.

PROTEIN SNACK PACK

· hard-boiled egg + prosciutto or ham + cheese cubes + hummus + mini pita + carrots

QUICK CAPRESE

· grape tomatoes + basil leaves + fresh torn mozzarella or bocconcini + olives + olive oil + sliced baguette

SAVORY YOGURT BOWL

· Greek yogurt + leftover roasted vegetables + cubes of cucumber + chopped nuts + herbs + cooked grains + salt + pepper

BREAKFAST FOR LUNCH

· granola + yogurt with honey + blueberries + almond butter on a homemade whole-grain waffle

CHIPS AND DIP

· tortilla chips + guacamole + Greek yogurt + black bean salsa + red pepper strips + cucumber coins + pineapple

Vanilla Cashew Ice-Cream Pops

WITH CHOCOLATE SHELL

There is a commercial ice-cream pop with a grandiose name and gold foil–lined package that I pick up as a picnic or post-lunch treat on summer weekends, and this is my reimagined, home-made, dairy-free version. I serve my rendition of the pop on the weekend when entertaining at lunchtime, as they're neither too heavy nor too sweet, and please adults and kids alike. They're the antithesis of a perfunctory lunchtime dessert.

I'm immensely proud of this recipe—the texture and taste are bang on. I believe it's worth purchasing an ice pop mold for these, but you will definitely make good use of it: I also use mine for smoothie pops, yogurt and fruit pops, homemade fudge pops, and more.

MAKES 4 LARGE OR 8 MINI   ⧗ 8 HOURS 25 MINUTES
⊕ 1 MONTH

1   For the ice-cream pops, add the cashews to a high-speed blender and pour in the just-boiled water, honey, coconut oil, vanilla, lemon juice, and salt. Cover and let sit for 10 minutes to allow the cashews to soften. Blend on high until the mixture is completely smooth, creamy, and liquefied, 20 to 30 seconds. Pour into a silicone ice pop mold (6 oz capacity or smaller, see the Lunch Note) or other ice pop mold, and slide in the sticks. Freeze until solid, at least 8 hours.

2   For the chocolate shell, line a plate or baking sheet (one that fits into your freezer) with parchment paper. Bring the frozen bars out of the freezer and release them from the mold. Add to the prepared plate or baking sheet and place them back in the freezer while melting the chocolate. In a small saucepan over low heat, melt the chocolate and coconut oil, and stir in the cocoa powder. Transfer the chocolate mixture to a tall glass

CONTINUED

**VANILLA CASHEW
ICE-CREAM POPS**

1 cup unsalted raw cashews

⅔ cup just-boiled water
    from the kettle

⅓ cup honey

¼ cup coconut oil

½ tsp vanilla extract

1 tsp lemon juice

¼ tsp salt

CHOCOLATE SHELL

1 cup semisweet chocolate
    chips or chopped dark
    chocolate

¼ cup coconut oil

1 Tbsp unsweetened cocoa
    powder, sifted

2 Tbsp toppings of choice
    (chopped nuts, cacao nibs,
    matcha, flaky salt, etc.)

measuring cup or heatproof drinking glass. Allow it to cool slightly so it's not too hot but remains liquid for dipping, about 10 minutes.

3   Working one at a time, dip the ice-cream pops into the chocolate (halfway or fully coated, to your preference), keeping each pop upside down until the chocolate shell has hardened, about 30 seconds. Place on the prepared baking sheet. Working one at a time again, with the remaining chocolate, drizzle thin streaks over the set chocolate and immediately sprinkle on your preferred toppings, to taste. Repeat with the remaining ice-cream pops, melted chocolate mixture (if you have leftover chocolate, dip peeled banana halves in it and freeze!), and toppings. Transfer back to the freezer until you are ready to serve. Store the pops in an airtight container in the freezer for up to 1 month.

★ ON ICE

To keep the pops from melting too quickly when serving (though, out of direct sunlight, they won't melt for up to 10 minutes), fill a large plate or shallow bowl with ice and cover it with plastic wrap. Place bars on the plastic wrap and bring them out to the table.

Ginger Kombucha–Baked Rhubarb Yogurt Parfaits

My mom's strawberry-rhubarb pie, baked until jammy and bubbling in her trademark flaky, ultra-rich pie crust and served with a scoop of vanilla ice cream, is something I can still taste—albeit imperfectly and only in my imagination—every time I see a lanky, hot-pink stalk of rhubarb. This is a simpler, lunch-friendly version of her pie, built a little differently. I've contrasted rhubarb's sour thwack with apples in place of strawberries (though you could certainly use strawberries if you want), and I use ginger kombucha for something a bit more modern to bake the fruit in, instead of the orange juice she used in her recipe. I realize the probiotic properties of the kombucha dissipate once heated, but it's the taste and syrupy quality I'm looking for here.

MAKES 4 TO 6   ⧖ 1 HOUR PLUS COOLING TIME
🕐 1 WEEK FOR GINGER KOMBUCHA–BAKED RHUBARB;
1 DAY FOR ASSEMBLED PARFAITS

½ cup ginger kombucha or ginger beer

¼ cup lightly packed dark brown sugar or coconut sugar

1 Tbsp finely chopped fresh ginger

1 Tbsp lemon juice

½ lb fresh rhubarb stalks, cut into 1-inch pieces, or chopped frozen rhubarb

2 apples, any variety, peeled and coarsely chopped

2–3 cups plain Greek yogurt, preferably whole milk, for serving

2–3 cups Maple, Lemon, and Ginger Granola (page 167) or prepared gluten-free granola, for serving

1   For the baked rhubarb, preheat the oven to 350°F. In a 9- × 13-inch glass or ceramic baking dish, combine the kombucha or ginger beer, sugar, ginger, and lemon juice. Add the rhubarb and apple, spreading it in a single layer. Cover tightly with foil and bake for 30 minutes, or until the fruit has fully collapsed. Mash it lightly with the back of a spoon, leaving some texture, and allow to cool slightly. If you are not using it immediately, store in an airtight container in the refrigerator for up to 1 week.

2   To assemble, divide the baked rhubarb among 4 to 6 small jars or containers (depending on how large a snack you'd like) and top with yogurt. Add the granola on top of the yogurt immediately before taking this to go, to retain crunch, or take a small ziplock baggie of granola alongside and top right before enjoying. If you are taking this to work, keep the yogurt and rhubarb refrigerated until you're ready to top it with the granola, if packed separately, and eat.

PART V

THE LUNCH LARDER

(stock up smartly)

THE FINAL PART of this book also happens to be a great place to begin. Use the following basic recipes, from condiments to grains to proteins, along with the gear recommendations, to breeze through your week, prepping and packing like a champ.

I turn to meal prep staples like plain roasted vegetables, basic whole grains, simply cooked proteins, and laid-back jar dressings for many reasons. If I haven't planned, have limited groceries, and very little time, they are a lifesaver. If I have planned, but am trying to satisfy different palates (mix and match to your heart's content), they are a lifesaver. If I'm looking to eat food without bells and whistles, maybe because that's just the mood I'm in, again they are a lifesaver.

You can turn staples into snacks, transform or add to leftovers to bulk up your meal, modify the seasonings, play by the seasons—these meal-prep must-haves are a blank canvas ready to be painted. But, if the following staple recipes aren't to your liking, consider picking components (vegetables, sauces, proteins, and grains) out of any number of recipes in the book, and tie them together for something a bit flashier. The idea of the modern lunch is to mix and match. It's contemporary, healthy, and an exciting way to cook and eat.

To aid you in making and storing your prepped meals and staple recipes, I've compiled a handy resource guide of equipment, from small kitchen appliances to single-serving containers to water bottles and more, so you can reach the level of lunch greatness I know you have in you. In my search for the best containers (leak-proof! BPA-free! dishwasher safe!), I was amazed at the number of options available now, which was absolutely not the case 10 years ago. Lunch is catching on in a big way. And if buying a new container (it doesn't need to be expensive) or kitchen tool encourages you to make, pack, and eat a homemade lunch, I say, go for it.

To make lunch a reality when it seems impossible, bookmark this section, for mini midday successes when you need them the most.

CHAPTER 11

Modern Meal Prep Staples

THIS CHAPTER IS FULL OF component recipes you'll want to keep on hand to create an entirely new lunch off the cuff, freshen up a recipe, or turn your jar, lunch box, tin, picnic basket, plate, platter, etc. on its head. From salad dressings to dips to whole grains, protein, and zippy quick pickles, these recipes are presented here, simply, for you.

Modern Staples

Dressings and Condiments

BALSAMIC VINAIGRETTE

In a medium-sized sealable glass jar, vigorously shake ½ cup of extra-virgin olive oil, ⅓ cup of balsamic vinegar, ¼ cup of apple cider (not vinegar) or apple juice, 2 tablespoons of Dijon mustard, 1 clove smashed garlic, ¼ teaspoon of salt, and ground black pepper to taste. Store in an airtight container in the refrigerator for up to 1 week. The oil will solidify once it is chilled, which is natural; 5 to 10 minutes outside the refrigerator will liquefy it again. Shake well before use.

BEET HORSERADISH RELISH

To a food processor, add 1 chopped beet (5½ ounces) and 4½ ounces (a 4-inch piece) of peeled and chopped fresh horse-radish; pulse until minced. Add ¼ cup of apple cider vinegar, 2 tablespoons of neutral oil (grapeseed, avocado, etc.) and 1 teaspoon of salt, and pulse again until a thick paste forms. Store in an airtight container in the refrigerator for up to 1 month (it loses heat as it ages).

CREAMY CAESAR DRESSING

In a medium bowl, combine 1 small clove of grated fresh garlic with ¼ cup of lemon juice; let sit for at least 10 minutes (this "cooks" the garlic, mellowing its raw pungency). Whisk in 1 cup of mayonnaise, 2 teaspoons of Worcestershire sauce (gluten-free and vegan, if desired), ¼ cup of finely grated parmesan or nutritional yeast, and ½ teaspoon of coarsely ground black pepper. Store in an airtight container in the refrigerator for up to 1 week.

FRENCH VINAIGRETTE

In a medium sealable glass jar, vigorously shake ½ cup of extra-virgin olive oil, 2 tablespoons of white wine vinegar or sherry vinegar, 2 tablespoons of Dijon mustard, 1 tablespoon of maple syrup, ½ teaspoon of dried thyme, ½ clove of minced garlic, ¼ teaspoon of salt, and ground black pepper to taste until combined. Store in an airtight container in the refrigerator for up to 1 week. The oil will solidify once it is chilled, which is natural; 5 to 10 minutes outside of the refrigerator will liquefy it again. Shake well before use.

GREEN GODDESS DRESSING

In a blender or food processor, combine ½ cup of buttermilk or kefir, ½ cup of mayonnaise, 2 tablespoons of lemon juice, 1 teaspoon of Worcestershire sauce (gluten-free and vegan, if needed), 1 cup of coarsely chopped fresh cilantro or parsley, ¼ cup of coarsely chopped fresh dill or mint, ¼ cup of sliced fresh basil, and 1 anchovy fillet (optional). Blend until smooth and pale green. Store in an airtight container in the refrigerator for up to 1 week. Shake well before use.

NUT BUTTER

Preheat the oven to 300°F. Add 3 cups of shelled, unsalted raw nuts (almonds, pecans, mixed, etc.) in a single layer to a large rimmed baking sheet. Roast for 25 to 30 minutes, until the nuts are fragrant and deep brown. Let cool completely. Transfer the cooled nuts to a food processor and blend, scraping down the sides once or twice, until the oils release and the nut butter is creamy. Store in an airtight container in the refrigerator for up to 1 month. Stir well before use.

SESAME ORANGE VINAIGRETTE

In a medium sealable glass jar, vigorously shake ¼ cup of orange juice, ¼ cup of neutral oil (grapeseed, avocado, etc.), 2 tablespoons of rice vinegar, 1 tablespoon of toasted sesame oil, 1 tablespoon of minced fresh ginger, ½ clove of minced garlic, and ¼ teaspoon of salt until combined. For a creamy variation, omit the salt and whisk in 1 to 2 tablespoons of white miso paste. Store in an airtight container in the refrigerator for up to 1 week. The oil will solidify once it is chilled, which is natural; 5 to 10 minutes outside of the refrigerator will liquefy it again. Shake well before use.

TAHINI-YOGURT DRESSING

In a medium bowl, add ⅔ cup of plain whole-milk yogurt, ½ cup of tahini, ¼ cup of lemon juice, and ¼ teaspoon of salt or

1 teaspoon of tamari and mix until combined. If a thinner dressing is desired, thin it with water, 1 tablespoon at a time. Store in an airtight container in the refrigerator for up to 1 week. Stir before use.

Proteins: Cook Your Own

BEANS AND LENTILS

STOVETOP BEANS If time allows, cover the beans with water and soak them overnight; drain and rinse well. Add 2 cups of dry or soaked beans to a large pot and cover them with 2 to 4 inches of fresh water. Bring to a boil, reduce the heat to medium-low, partially cover, and cook until tender (top up with water during cooking if the beans are no longer submerged); this can take anywhere from 1 hour to 2 hours. Drain, rinse, and cool. Store in 2-cup portions in a ziplock baggie in the freezer for up to 3 months.

PRESSURE COOKER BEANS This is the quickest method of cooking beans at home, taking under 40 minutes. To cook, follow the manufacturer's instructions for your pressure cooker. Then drain, rinse, and cool the beans and store them in 2-cup portions in a ziplock baggie in the freezer for up to 3 months.

STOVETOP LENTILS Add 1 cup of lentils (not split red lentils, which stew down) to a large pot and cover with at least 4 inches of water. Bring to a boil, reduce the heat to medium-low, and cook, partially covered, for 15 to 30 minutes, depending on the lentil variety, until tender but not falling apart. Drain, cool, and store in an airtight container in the refrigerator for up to 1 week. I don't recommend cooking lentils with a pressure cooker, as they turn very mushy.

HARD-BOILED EGGS

To a large pot or medium saucepan, add as many eggs as you can fit snugly in a single bottom layer and cover with at least 2 inches of water. Bring to a boil, cover, and remove from heat. Let eggs stand, covered, for 10 to 12 minutes. Drain, rinse with cold water, and refrigerate until you are ready to use. Keep them in their shells for easy transport and optimal freshness, and peel just before eating. Recycle an empty egg carton and label it "HB" with a permanent maker, and keep your hard-boiled eggs in that—this way there's no confusion when you open the refrigerator.

SALMON FILLET (SKINLESS, BONELESS)

Preheat the oven to 400°F. Line a large rimmed baking sheet with parchment paper, add the salmon, season it with salt and pepper, and roast for 12 to 15 minutes, or until the salmon is firm but flakes easily. Don't overcook it or it will become dry. Cool and store in an airtight container in the refrigerator for up to 3 days. If you using salmon with skin, discard the skin after cooking before storing.

CHICKEN BREAST (SKINLESS, BONELESS)

For extra flavor before roasting or grilling chicken (skip for poaching), marinate it in a mixture of yogurt, lemon juice, olive oil, fresh herbs, garlic, salt, and pepper for up to 1 day. Or marinate in any of the dressing recipes in this book for up to 1 day.

GRILLED Heat a grill or grill pan to medium-high heat. Coat the chicken in olive oil and season it with salt and pepper. Grill for 5 to 6 minutes per side, until the juices run clear and the thickest part of the chicken reads 160°F to 165°F on a meat thermometer. Rest for 5 minutes if slicing or shredding. Store in an airtight container in the refrigerator for up to 5 days.

POACHED Bring a large pot of water to a boil. Salt well, add any aromatics you like (herbs, garlic, ginger, lemon, etc.), and reduce to a very gentle simmer with only a few bubbles present. Add the chicken and poach until tender and cooked through (do not rapidly boil or the chicken will toughen), 10 to 12 minutes. When done, the chicken should be opaque white throughout with clear juices, and the thickest part should read 160°F to 165°F on a meat thermometer. Rest for 5 minutes before slicing or shredding. Store in an airtight container in the refrigerator for up to 5 days.

ROASTED Preheat the oven to 375°F. Line a large rimmed baking sheet with parchment paper, add the chicken, drizzle with olive oil to coat, season with salt and pepper, and roast for 15 to 20 minutes, until the juices run clear and no pink is left in the flesh, and the thickest part of chicken reads 160°F to 165°F on a meat thermometer. Rest for 5 minutes before slicing or shredding. Store in an airtight container in the refrigerator for up to 5 days.

STEAK (EG. FLANK, SKIRT, SIRLOIN)

For extra flavor before searing or grilling, marinate the steak in a mixture of red wine, olive oil, fresh rosemary or thyme, garlic, salt, and pepper for 30 minutes to 2 hours. Or dress the beef once cooked, rested, and sliced, with any of the dressing recipes in this book.

SEARED OR GRILLED STEAK (½ INCH THICK)
Take the steak out of the refrigerator for at least 15 minutes before cooking. Heat a cast-iron skillet (my preference) or grill pan over medium-high heat. If you've marinated your steak, pat off the excess marinade with a paper towel to dry the surface, ensuring a crispy crust. Season the steak with salt and pepper. Wipe the skillet or grill pan with a thin layer of high-temperature oil, such as avocado oil. Cook the steak for 2½ to 3 minutes per side for medium-rare or 3 to 5 minutes per side for well done (adjust the cooking times according to thickness). Transfer to a plate and rest for at least 5 minutes, and preferably 10, before slicing against the grain (crosswise) into strips as thick or thin as you like. Store in an airtight container in the refrigerator for up to 5 days.

Proteins: Ready to Go

· Canned sardines packed in olive oil or water

· Canned tuna packed in olive oil or water

· Hot-smoked or cured salmon, trout, or mackerel

· Sushi-grade raw salmon or tuna

· Last night's leftover chicken, pork tenderloin, steak, meatballs, salmon, shrimp, tuna, turkey burger patties, etc.

· Canned beans and legumes

- Prepared hummus

- Greek yogurt

- Smoked tofu or extra-firm tofu

- Nut butters or seed butters

- Hemp hearts, pumpkin seeds, almonds, or cashews

Grains

Grains can be made on the stovetop, in a pressure cooker, or in a rice cooker. I've provided directions for stovetop only. Follow the manufacturer's instructions for pressure cooker or rice cooker grains, and see specific product recommendations in the Gear Guide (page 245).

BARLEY   To a medium saucepan, add 1 cup of barley and cover with 4 inches of water. Bring to a boil, reduce to a simmer, partially cover, and cook for 25 minutes, or until the grains are tender. Drain well and transfer to a large container, cool, seal, and store in the refrigerator for up to 5 days.

BROWN RICE (LONG GRAIN)   In a medium saucepan, bring 1⅔ cups of water and 1 cup of long-grain brown rice to a boil, reduce to a simmer, cover (or partially cover for a few minutes to keep it from boiling over), and cook for 55 minutes. Remove from heat and steam, covered, for 5 minutes. Fluff with a fork, transfer to a large container, cool, seal, and store in the refrigerator for up to 5 days.

BROWN RICE (SHORT GRAIN)   In a medium saucepan, bring 1¾ cups of water and 1 cup of short-grain brown rice to a boil, reduce to a simmer, cover (or partially cover for a few minutes to keep it from boiling over), and cook for 55 minutes. Remove from heat and steam, covered, for 5 minutes. Fluff with a fork, transfer to a large container, cool, seal, and store in the refrigerator for up to 5 days.

COUSCOUS   In a medium saucepan, bring 1 cup of water or broth to a boil. Remove from the heat and add 1 cup of instant couscous and ¼ teaspoon of salt. Stir, cover, and set aside to rehydrate for 10 minutes. Fluff with a fork, transfer to a large container, cool, seal, and store in the refrigerator for up to 5 days.

FARRO   To a medium saucepan, add 1 cup of farro and cover with 3 to 4 inches of water. Bring to a boil, reduce the heat to medium-low, and simmer for 25 to 35 minutes, or until tender. Drain, rinse with cold water, and drain again. Transfer to a large container, cool, seal, and store in the refrigerator for up to 5 days.

OAT GROATS   To a medium saucepan, add ½ cup of oat groats (for 2 cups cooked) and cover with 3 to 4 inches of water. Bring to a boil, reduce to a simmer, cover (or partially cover for a few minutes to keep it from boiling over), and cook for 35 to 50 minutes (different brands take more or less time), until tender. Drain, rinse with cold water, and drain again. Transfer to a large container, cool, seal, and store in the refrigerator for up to 5 days.

QUINOA   In a medium saucepan, bring 2 cups of water and 1 cup of quinoa to a boil. Reduce to a simmer, cover (or partially cover for a few minutes to keep it from boiling over) and cook for 15 minutes. Remove from the heat and let sit, covered, for 5 minutes. Fluff with a fork, transfer to a large container, cool, seal, and store in the refrigerator for up to 5 days.

Vegetables

ROASTED VEGETABLES   For every pound of vegetables cut into ½- to 1-inch cubes, toss with 1 tablespoon of extra-virgin olive oil, ¼ teaspoon of salt, and ½ teaspoon of dried herbs or spices of choice, more to taste. Roast at 375°F for 15 to 45 minutes, depending on the vegetable (for example, broccoli roasts far more quickly than squash), until tender and brown around the edges. Let cool completely and store in an airtight container in the refrigerator for up 5 days.

Vegetables that love to be roasted include squash (eg., peeled butternut, skin-on delicata, peeled kabocha), sweet potatoes, baby potatoes, Brussels sprouts, radishes, zucchinis, onions, beets, carrots, parsnips, rutabaga, celery root, turnips, broccoli, cauliflower, and kale.

If you are using a mixture of vegetables, stage their cooking times so you don't overcook and undercook the entire tray. For instance, if you're making a tray of roasted sweet potatoes and kale, start by roasting the sweet potatoes until they are tender and caramelized, which takes about 30 to 35 minutes for medium pieces. Then toss in the kale, which will roast and crisp up in just a few minutes.

PICKLED RED ONIONS   Slice 1 red onion into paper-thin half-moons with a knife, a mandolin, or the slicing attachment of a food processor; add to a large glass jar with a tight-fitting lid. In a medium saucepan, bring 1 cup of water, 1 cup of distilled white vinegar, and 1 tablespoon of honey or granulated sugar to a boil. Once boiling, pour the hot mixture over the onion to cover completely. Seal and cool to room temperature. Store in the refrigerator for up to 1 month.

I use pickled red onions in salads (they're especially nice in a radicchio, apple, and toasted pecan salad, or on top of a classic creamy Caesar), on grain bowls, on cheese platters, on top of soups and chilis, tucked into a pita with hummus, on avocado toast, and in black bean tacos.

CHAPTER 12

Gear Guide

AT ITS MOST MINIMALISTIC, preparing and packing lunch requires only a basic kitchen, two sizes of containers or screw-top jars—which are as well-suited for the workplace as they are for an intimate picnic— utensils, and a tote bag. The following are simply products I've tested while developing, plating, and packing the recipes for this book. And, like the recipes, I aim to give you options—there's bound to be at least one tool that appeals to you here.

Gear Guide

Portable Containers and Food Wraps

- Bee's Wrap (food wrap): http://www.beeswrap.com
- Black + Blum: https://www.boxappetit.com
- ECOLunchbox: https://ecolunchboxes.com
- Glasslock: http://glasslockusa.com
- IKEA: http://www.ikea.com
- Indigo: https://www.chapters.indigo.ca
- LunchBots: http://www.lunchbots.com
- Monbento: http://us.monbento.com/en
- President's Choice: https://www.loblaws.ca
- Rubbermaid: http://www.rubbermaid.com
- Russbe: http://www.russbe.com
- Starfrit: https://www.starfrit.com
- Takenaka: https://www.takenaka-global.com

Jars

- Ball: https://www.freshpreserving.com
- IKEA: http://www.ikea.com/ca/en/catalog/categories/ departments/small_storage/15937
- Le Parfait: http://www.leparfait.com
- Weck: http://www.weckjars.com/products.php

Thermal Containers

- Black + Blum: https://www.boxappetit.com
- LunchBots: http://www.lunchbots.com
- Thermos: http://www.thermos.com/product_catalog. aspx?CatCode=FOOD

Meal Prep Storage

- Bee's Wrap (food wrap): http://www.beeswrap.com
- Glasslock: http://glasslockusa.com

- IKEA: http://www.ikea.com
- President's Choice: https://www.loblaws.ca
- Rubbermaid: http://www.rubbermaid.com
- Starfrit: https://www.starfrit.com

Small Appliances

- Blender: Blendtec: http://www.blendtec.com
- Blender: Vitamix: https://www.vitamix.com/ca/en_us
- Food processor: Cuisinart: http://www.cuisinart.ca
- Kitchen scale: Starfrit: https://www.starfrit.com/en/electronic-scale-quartz-model
- Pressure cooker: Instant Pot: http://instantpot.com
- Slow cooker: Breville: https://www.breville.ca/the-fast-slow-pro-tm.html

Water Bottles

- Black + Blum: https://www.boxappetit.com
- Indigo: https://www.chapters.indigo.ca
- Kate Spade: https://www.katespade.com
- S'well: https://www.swellbottle.com

Lunch Bags, Totes, and Picnic Baskets

- BAGGU: https://baggu.com
- Barebones Living: http://www.barebonesliving.com/c/10/Coolers
- Bed Bath & Beyond: https://www.bedbathandbeyond.com
- Built NY: http://www.builtny.com
- Indigo: https://www.chapters.indigo.ca
- Kate Spade: https://www.katespade.com
- L.L. Bean: https://www.llbean.com
- Takenaka: https://www.takenaka-global.com
- Wayfair: https://www.wayfair.ca

Coolers

- Barebones Living: http://www.barebonesliving.com/c/10/Coolers
- Coleman: http://www.coleman.com/coleman-coolersandwaterjugs
- Yeti: http://intl.yeti.com

Beverage Making

- Coffee, burr grinder: Baratza Virtuoso https://www.baratza.com
- Coffee, gooseneck pour-over kettle: Fellow Stagg Pour-Over Kettle (electric and stovetop) http://fellowproducts.com/stagg/
- Coffee, pour-over: Fellow Stagg Pour Over Dripper http://fellowproducts.com/shop/staggdripper/
- Coffee, pour-over: Hario v60 http://www.hario.jp/index.html
- Kitchen scale: Starfrit https://www.starfrit.com/en/electronic-scale-quartz-model

Plates and Platters

- CB2: https://www.cb2.com
- IKEA: http://www.ikea.com/ca/en
- Indigo: https://www.chapters.indigo.ca/en-ca
- Small-batch ceramicists: https://www.etsy.com

Drinking Glasses

- Duralex: https://www.duralexusa.com
- La Rochere: https://www.larochere-na.com
- Loliware Biodegr(edible) Cups: https://www.loliware.com
- Riedel: https://riedelcanada.ca

Acknowledgments

TO GEOFF WOODLEY, my guy, who supported me throughout the entire cookbook-creating process, from when it was just an idea floating around our living room until it was a real book to hold. You're my favorite person (in general and) to cook for and with. Thanks for your many hours of helping me with my proposal, prop shopping, grocery buying, brainstorming design ideas, and photography, and for eating lunch for dinner for several months in a row as I powered through the recipe testing phase. I know you're always there to cheer me on. Thank you.

To my literary agent, Carly Watters, your guidance and business wisdom continue to amaze and inform me, and your attention to and understanding of this project (our third together!) helped me focus and thrive. I'm so happy to have you and P.S. Literary Agency on my side. Thank you.

To Bhavna Chauhan, my editor, who is one of the most brilliant, beautiful, funny, and encouraging women I've ever met and, I hope, a friend for life. You "got" this book (and me) from the very beginning and trusted me to be my creative self. Thank you.

To Robert McCullough and the Appetite by Random House and Penguin Random House Canada crew, for your support, approval, and passion for my cookbook. Your drive and excitement to make and spread the word about truly awesome books inspires me. I'm thrilled to be at home there. Thank you all.

To Jen Griffiths, my ace book designer, whom I've been on the same page with since our first meeting. You somehow read my mind, designing the book I've always dreamed of. You're so talented and I'm so lucky. Thank you.

To my yummybeet.com community and cookbook readers, your support makes it possible for me to do what I love. The positive space you've helped create brings me a ton of happiness, every single day. It was your photos of my recipes, cooked by you, how you tweaked and made them your own, brought them for lunch, and meal-prepped them for the busy week ahead that inspired *Modern Lunch* (really!). Thank you.

To my family, the Days, Dad, Kirsten, Stewart, Katie, Chloe, and Ava, for your love, emotional support, and excitement. I have the best family in the world. And to my new family, the Woodleys, Jane, John, and Laura, for your hugs, interest, love of food, and love of me. Thank you all.

And to my friends, for making me laugh, encouraging me, and bringing tons of fun to my life. Thank you.

Index